iner Tippetts,
its harbour
4.

A HISTORY OF ILFRACOMBE

A History of
ILFRACOMBE

Lois Lamplugh

Phillimore

1984

Published by
PHILLIMORE & CO. LTD.
Shopwyke Hall, Chichester, Sussex

ISBN 0 85033 525 6

Printed and bound in Great Britain by
THE CAMELOT PRESS
Southampton, Hants.

CONTENTS

LIST OF TEXT ILLUSTRATIONS

LIST OF PLATES

(between pages 84 and 85)

ACKNOWLEDGEMENTS

In writing this account of Ilfracombe's past I have again, as in the case of my earlier book, *Barnstaple: Town on the Taw,* made repeated use of the library of the North Devon Athenaeum, Barnstaple, and have been grateful for the helpfulness of Mr. J. M. Rowe, Head Librarian, and his staff. I would also like to thank the past and present Curators of the Ilfracombe Museum, Mr. John Longhurst and Mrs. Joy Slocombe, for allowing me to consult documents and early guide books held by the Museum, as well as its extensive file of photographs: a number of the latter (see below) are reproduced here by kind permission of the Trustees of the Museum. My thanks are due also to the following: the librarians and staff of the Reference Library and Public Library, Barnstaple; the West Country Studies Library, and the Devon Record Office; to Lt.-Col. G. S. Incledon-Webber for allowing me to quote from a diary kept by his ancestor, Philip Rogers Webber; to Mr. Peter Ferguson for giving me information concerning the *Snowflake;* to Mr. Mervyn C. Dalling and Mr. John Kinsman for lending photographs. The kindness of all those who lent or offered to lend copies of songs by H. Verne and Allen T. Hussell is acknowledged in the Appendix, in which some of the songs are reproduced.

*   *   *   *   *

PICTORIAL ACKNOWLEDGEMENTS

I should like to thank the following for providing text illustrations and/or photographs for the book: the North Devon Athenaeum for text illustrations 1, 4, 17, 18, 19, 24 and 32, and plates 4, 6, 12, 13, 19, 20 and 32; the Trustees of Ilfracombe Museum for text illustrations 2, 3, 5, 6, 7, 8, 9, 10, 11, 14, 15, 16, 21, 22, 23, 25, 26, 27, 28, 29, 31 and 34, and plates 1, 5, 7, 9, 11, 15, 16, 18, 23, 24, 25, 26, 27, 28, 29, 30 and 31; John Kinsman for plates 2, 10, 14, 17, 21, 22; and Mervyn C. Dalling for plates 3 and 27.

Chapter One

PEOPLE OF THE SEA AND LAND

AS DEVON GAVE ITS NAME to certain ancient rocks, so Ilfracombe gave its name to a wide band of a variety of these rocks, the Ilfracombe Beds, running inland from the coast to the Brendon Hills. Between the valley of the Taw and the north coast there are several such bands, lying more or less parallel: Pickwell Down Beds, Morte Slates, Hangman Grits, and so on. All are types of limestone, sandstone, slate and grit formed in the shallow seas that covered what are now the southern counties of England during the geological period known, by derivation, as the Devonian period, estimated as lasting from about 400 million to 350 million years ago.

Much nearer our own time—recent estimates have put it at no more than some six or seven thousand years ago—the outlines of the British Isles had settled into something resembling those of today, although, because sea levels were then still considerably lower, each island was larger. At that period, what are now the cliffs of north Devon would have appeared as a long inland escarpment, the northern face of hills rising several miles from the sea. But gradually the climate began to grow warmer; a slow enormous thaw melted ice to raise sea levels and drown long stretches of coastal lands.

Small groups of people lived on and around Exmoor during this era of rising seas, but can be known only from the largely haphazard finds of objects they made or used; not a great deal of systematic archaeological work has been done in the region. They left behind faint traces of their lives in tools and weapons of stone, copper and bronze, and more substantial traces of their deaths in burial chambers and round barrows.

Commanding Ilfracombe to the east is the great head of Hillsborough, 450 feet above the sea, so impressive that some 19th-century visitors referred to it as a mountain. No one knows just when it first became a place of human habitation. It is possible that the Bronze Age people came here, or at least buried their dead here; what was identified as a Bronze Age cist was discovered on the site by chance in the 1930s. Workmen unearthed it when digging a trench to stop the spread of a gorse fire. The founder and curator of the Ilfracombe museum, Mervyn Palmer, tried to persuade the council to preserve it, without success; the cist was buried again.

But from about 100 B.C. some of the Iron Age Celts known as the Dumnonii— said to mean 'people of the land'—had moved into this area, and left on the landscape more conspicuous marks of their settlements than their predecessors

1

1. A print from W.B. Cooke's *Picturesque Views on the South Coast of England*, a collection of engravings from water colours made by J.M.W. Turner, published by J. & A. Arch, London, in 1826. Turner's own title for this painting—made about 1811—was 'Ilfracombe, Storm and Shipwreck'. (see pp.45-6.)

had done. These were the earthworks of their hill forts and cliff castles. One group of the Dumnonii may well have chosen to settle overlooking the site of the future Ilfracombe because of that useful geological accident, the outcrop of rock sheltering a sandy beach from which small boats could be launched. Around the crest of the hill they built a defended settlement. The grass- and gorse-covered walls of this fort on Hillsborough can still be made out. It has been called 'a really fine example of the Cornish type of cliff castle, the only one known on greater Exmoor unless the great earthwork on Wind Hill (Countisbury) be included in the category'.[1]

If it had not been abandoned by the first century A.D., it inhabitants may have watched ships from the Mediterranean passing up-Channel. The Romans, finding the Silures of South Wales troublesome, built fortlets to keep watch on them, first at Old Burrow, near what is now County Gate, and later at Martinhoe on a hill between Heddon's Mouth and Woody Bay. It has been suggested that the establishment and later maintenance of these forts was much more likely to have been by sea than across country, in spite of the Roman presence at *Isca Dumnoniorum* (Exeter), though such isolated garrisons would have needed to be on friendly terms with neighbouring people.[2]

Gradually, in the centuries after Roman troops had been withdrawn from Britain, Saxons made their way westwards into Devon, and had probably begun to establish homesteads in the north of the county by the last quarter of the seventh century. It is not until the Domesday survey was taken in 1086, however, that we are given a name approximating to Ilfracombe, Alfreincoma. This is said to signify the combe of the sons of Alfred. Antiquarians used to try to link it with Alfred, king of Wessex, but today's place-name historians do not. It has been pointed out that places in Saxon times were not 'named after great men or famous kings, but after early owners . . . who set up farms and worked them with success'; there are many names of the 'Alf' type, and in any case, the name of a settlement such as Ilfracombe may have been fixed a century before the time of Alfred the Great.[3] But whatever the identity of the man who first chose to settle in the shelter of the seven-crested ridge of the Torrs, it may be imagined that he pastured his animals in the meadows bordering the confluence of the East and West Wilder brooks, and ploughed the lower slopes of Bicclescombe for corn. But at the same time he was possibly influenced, as his Celtic fore-runners may have been, by the nearness of a rock-protected beach offering a little natural harbour.

His successor at the time of the Conquest was called Ailmar or Elmer; he paid geld, or tax, on one hide of land, usually regarded as equalling 120 acres. Ailmar's neighbour at Hagginton to the east, Ulf, also paid tax on one hide— but it is interesting to note that Brismer, at Lincombe to the west, paid tax on a property twice as big: the manor farm of Ilfracombe was smaller than the manor farm of Lincombe. In 1066 or soon after, these Saxon landowners, like their fellows all over England, were dispossessed, and their fate cannot be known: the Norman clerks did not trouble to record what became of them. William of Normandy gave Ilfracombe, Lincombe and Hagginton, among many other possessions, to one of his followers whom he had appointed Sheriff of Devon, Baldwin de Brionne. (Hele, as well as Higher and Lower Warcombe, went not to Baldwin but to form a small part of the extensive estates of the powerful and bellicose Bishop of Coutances.)

Most of the Norman lords who received large, scattered grants of land in effect sub-let them, on feudal terms. Ilfracombe, with Lincombe, Hagginton, Middle Marwood and Heanton Punchardon, went to a Norman called Robert, who is sometimes referred to as Robert of Punchardon (a name latinised as Ponte Cardonis.)

Of the 480 or so acres of Ilfracombe and its two adjoining holdings, 250 acres were pasture. The Exeter Book of Domesday shows us that on these acres Robert ran 333 sheep, more than a dozen cattle, and kept a couple of horses. Surprisingly, since one might have expected the valleys to be tree-covered even then, there is no mention of woodland in the entries for the three farms; perhaps this is why a total of only 31 pigs was reported. The properties were fairly valuable, being worth in all £10 a year, then a substantial amount. On the Ilfracombe manor there were 12 villagers, 12 small-holders and five slaves; if each of these was the head of a family, this might indicate a population of rather more than 100 people, excluding the family and retainers of Robert or, if he lived elsewhere, his steward.

By 1166 the little group of five manors was in the hands of Robert Fitzroy, the illegitimate son of William of Normandy, who was Baron of Okehampton. From him they were held by Henry de Campo Arnulfi or Champernowne. The Champernownes came from Cambernon, near Coutances, in Normandy. A knight named 'de Cambernon' was among those present in the Battle of Hastings; it has been suggested that he arrived in England in the train of the Bishop of Coutances and was rewarded with grants from the lands allotted to the bishop. Champernownes were later to hold manors in several parts of Devon, as well as some in Cornwall.[4]

However, the first of the name to settle in Ilfracombe was Jordan de Cambernon, who was born in 1093. His name appears as a witness to two grants made by members of the de Tracy family, lords of the manor of Barnstaple, between 1129 and 1148. He linked himself with his feudal lord, Robert Fitzroy, by marrying his daughter, Mabira, referred to as 'Lady of Maisoncelles'. On Jordan's death his younger son, Henry, mentioned above, inherited Ilfracombe; his descendants continued to hold it for a considerable time.

There was soon to be a second manor of Ilfracombe: a 'borough manor' had come into existence by 1249.[5] Reichel says that it was evidently carved out of the Domesday manor at an early date. By 1274 it was held by Henry de Tracy, lord of Barnstaple, from Henry de Champernowne, at a yearly rent of eight marks. Possibly at the request of his tenant, Champernowne obtained a grant in 1278 to hold a market every Monday, and an annual fair lasting three days. When later lords of Barnstaple died—for instance, Geoffrey de Camville in 1308, and William Martyn in 1326—the rent for this 'moiety of a manor' had not changed. In the latter year, there were 49 burgesses. The borough had no mayor; its affairs were governed by a portreeve.[6]

2. It is probable that a church of some kind stood on the site from Saxon times; the base of the stone-built tower may be Saxon, but is more probably Norman. This view, painted from the Old Barnstaple Road by W. Gauci, c.1835, is slightly misleading, giving the impression that the church lies on the lower slopes of the Torrs, instead of on a hillock with the valley of the West Wilder Brook beyond.

During the 14th century, and almost certainly earlier, the people of Ilfracombe indulged in the not uncommon medieval practise of holding their fairs in the churchyard. In 1384 Bishop Brantynghame of Exeter deplored the custom, and decreed that it must stop. Possibly his order was ignored: certainly there was trouble the following year when some kind of riotous fracas resulted in the shedding of human blood in the churchyard, necessitating a ceremony of purification.

It is probable that in Saxon times there had been a small timber church on the hill where today's parish church of the Holy Trinity stands. It has been suggested that either the Saxons or the Normans built a stone tower there, originally intended for defence (to the Normans, the small steep hillock would have offered a ready-made motte), this being incorporated in the later stone church.[7] The first incumbent whose name survives was Oliver, one of the de Tracys of Barnstaple, who was instituted in June 1263. The Champernownes held the patronage of the living, and members of the family were sometimes appointed to it. Henry de Campo Arnulfi (or Monteforti, another Latinised form of the name Champernowne) succeeded Oliver de Tracy in 1272.

A later clerical Champernowne got into debt, and the entry concerning this in the Exeter Ecclesiastical Register, in 1320, gives an early example of a spelling of the town's name which, at a time when such variants as 'Elvertecoumbe' and

3. At any time from the 14th century onwards a walker or look-out on the northern slopes of the Capstone would have seen the Chapel of St Nicholas on Lantern Hill, with Hillsborough beyond, looking much as they do here, although the walkway or parade was not cut until 1843. From *Twenty-Four Views of Ilfracombe* by J. Gadsby (n.d., c.1875).

'Ylfredecumbe' were to be found in documents, is surprisingly close to the present one. A writ had been received from London, the register noted, 'concerning a debt of Reginald Chambron, parson of Ilfrecombe, of forty shillings, due to Arnold de Boweys'. In reply, Exeter observed 'There is not in our diocese a Reginald Chambron of *Ilfrecombe*; however Reginald de Chambernoun, parson of the Church of Ilfardcombe, has been distrained to the value of one mark'. Reginald de Champernoun, in fact, may have been inclined to run into financial difficulties. Not only is he known to have been dunned for debt, but he clearly spent nothing on his parsonage house. When his relation—possibly his nephew—John de Champernoun succeeded him as rector in August 1333, he complained that he had found the house and premises in a very dilapidated state, and had incurred considerable expense in repairs and improvements.

Walter Stapledon, bishop of Exeter, visited Ilfracombe in November 1321. Evidently the town's population had been rising fairly rapidly; the bishop declared in the presence of Reginald de Champernoun, or Champernowne, his father, Sir Henry, and a gathering of parishioners, that the size of the church was utterly inadequate to the needs of its congregation. He commanded that the nave and aisles should be extended by at least 24 feet. The work was to be carried out within two years from the following Michaelmas, and the penalty for failure to comply was £40, the equivalent of many thousands of pounds today.

The relevant entry in the Ecclesiastical Register gives the names of 18 of the parishioners, who would have been the local men of most consequence. The names are partly Latinised (in the usual medieval fashion), so that Adam and Joel Smith become 'Adami and Johelis Fabri', and John and Thomas Baker become 'Johannis and Thome Pistoris'; and partly Gallicised—so that we have 'Wilhelmi le Tailleur' and 'Johannis le Lange'.[8]

The work on the church was duly carried out, within the time limit. In fact the parishioners, perhaps determined to show the bishop what they were capable of, made the building a good deal larger than he had required. It is supposed that they completely rebuilt it, so that the present church of the Holy Trinity is basically of early 14th-century origin, although, of course, many changes have been made to its fabric over the centuries. (Only a century later, in 1436, indulgences were twice granted for substantial alterations.)[9] The Revd. Frank Nesbitt, in his history of the church, says that two aisles extending the full length of the nave were added, the chancel replaced and lengthened by 24 feet, and Allen Hussell in his *North Devon Churches,* gives a full account of the way the old defensive tower may have been incorporated in the new church. He supposed it to have been taken down above the present ground storey 'the old stones being re-used, the walls built battering and the tower probably finished with a low timber spire, covered with lead or oak shingling'. However, the existing battlemented parapet and the pinnacles are of late 15th-century work. Any traces of Saxon 'long and short work' at the quoins of the ground storey would long ago have been obliterated, since the facings of the tower have been considerably repaired from time to time.

Four chapels were dependent on the church. Three of them were outside
Ilfracombe itself, at Westercombe, West Hagginton and Lee, but the fourth was
the little chapel on Lantern Hill, above the harbour, which was dedicated to St
Nicholas, patron saint of sailors and of scholars. It has been suggested that the
priest may have taught local boys, and this could have been true if it was from the
beginning a chantry chapel with its own priest, but it seems that the rector (as
he was until 1546) of the parish usually officiated there. Certainly when the
chapel first appears by name in the Exeter Ecclesiastical Registers in 1416, Bishop
Stafford was licensing Hugh Herle, whom he had newly instituted as rector of
Ilfracombe, to celebrate in the chapels of both St Nicholas and St Wardrede
at Lee, on their festivals, for one year. By that time, St Nicholas's chapel may
have been about 100 years old: experts in ecclesiastical architecture have
estimated that it was built at some date between 1300 and 1325—possibly at
the time that the parish church was being enlarged, after the visit of Bishop
Stapledon.

The Ecclesiastical Registers provide two other sidelights on the chapel's
history. In 1419 Bishop Lacy granted an indulgence of 40 days to all true
penitents who made a pilgrimage there ('Doubtless', says the Revd. Nesbitt,
'they were not expected to come with empty hands') and in the next century
Bishop Veysey made the same offer to penitents who contributed to the
maintenance of the light that year by year, as he put it, sparkled brightly, like
a star, through all the nights of winter, from the highest point of the chapel above
the harbour of Ilfracombe.[10] Unfortunately it is impossible to know when the
chapel had first begun to double as a lighthouse, and, in fact, it has been
conjectured that some kind of beacon was lit on the hill on winter nights even
before there was a chapel there.

Both Risdon and Westcote, writing in the early part of the 17th century,
mention what the latter calls 'a continual pharos', but neither notes that it was
maintained in the chapel. However, it continued to be lit in winter long after the
dissolution of all chantry chapels, and after the original purpose of the building
was for a while forgotten. Early in the 19th century a writer expressed surprise
that Ilfracombe should have built its lighthouse in the form of a chapel; another
remarked that it wore 'every appearance of having been a chapel; but no trace
of its origin is to be found'.

It is about a mile from the church on its hillock to the chapel on its wave-
washed rock. The church, if it was Saxon in origin, may have formed a focus
for the life of an inland pastoral settlement, the original manor, four centuries
before the chapel was set to watch over the harbour. How soon the two were
loosely linked by an irregular line of small dwellings studded along a ledge on
the north-facing slope between them cannot be known; by the early 17th century
the town consisted of 'one street lying scatteringly'. But from the time of the
Norman kings, it was the harbour that gave the town its character.

Chapter Two

A MEDIEVAL PORT

FOR CENTURIES, Ilfracombe was used as a port of embarkation for Ireland. It first appears in this role in the reign of King John, who in 1208 ordered men and ships from Wales to gather there to transport soldiers across the Irish Channel, and later in the 13th century Henry III directed a similar fleet to assemble, also bound for Ireland. Three hundred years later still, in the reign of Elizabeth I, quite large drafts of soldiers—up to 800 at a time—were sent to Ilfracombe, by way of Barnstaple, to take ship as reinforcements for the Irish wars.

During the early part of the 14th century, demands were made on the town—which was still an independent port: it did not become subject to the port of Exeter until the reign of Richard II—to provide ships for the king's service. In 1302 Edward I ordered Ilfracombe and Barnstaple together to supply one ship to assist in his war against the Scots; nine years later Edward II required 'Ilfardcumme with Briggewauter and Bardestaple' to send three ships to assist in his attempt to defeat 'Robert le Brus'. Edward III's demands were more extensive. At the time when he was planning the siege of Calais, he required maritime towns to send representatives to London to discuss matters. Ilfracombe duly sent two burgesses from its borough manor. They may well have been surprised to hear the size of the armada the king was planning to assemble (some 750 ships and 15,000 men), and even more so to learn the contribution expected of their own town. Various transcripts, made between 1575 and 1630, survive of what was, according to one of them, 'The rolle of the huge ffleete of Ed 3 before Callice . . . whereby appeareth the wonderfull strengthe of England by sea in those days'. They show some discrepancies in numbers, but at least three agree in stating that Ilfracombe sent six ships and 79 men. (According to Professor Hoskins, the copy of the roll at Cruwys Morchard House has eight ships and 62 men).[1] This compares with seven ships and 120 men from 'Tawmouth', which would have included Barnstaple, Bideford and Appledore. Since 1822, when the Lysons' *Magna Britannia* appeared, containing the statement that Ilfracombe contributed six ships and not 79, but 82 mariners to the fleet destined for the expedition to Calais, there can have been no guide book that has omitted to boast of this proof of the town's former maritime importance.

Certainly the figures (whichever is correct) indicate that the Ilfracombe of the last decades before the Black Death was regarded as a reasonably prosperous and populous place. Bishop Stapledon's order for the enlarging of the church, and the fact that the parishioners exceeded his suggested measurements, may be looked

9

on as supporting evidence. However, the lay subsidy rolls of 1332 indicate that the townspeople were by no means wealthy. The lay subsidies (clergy were taxed separately) were taxes on movable goods, and had been raised at intervals since the time of Henry III. In Ilfracombe only 33 people (one of them a woman, Alice Wolde) owned enough property to be taxed, and the amount payable by each individual was not large, even by contemporary standards: there were three men paying two shillings—including the lord of the manor, William Champernoun, whose name heads the list—and sums of anything from eightpence to 1s. 8d. were required of all the others. Turning to Barnstaple's tax list, one finds 99 people eligible for tax, with the general level in the range of 2s. 6d. to six shillings. The total for Barnstaple was roughly ten times that for Ilfracombe. Even allowing for Barnstaple's larger population, the relative demands made on each town for the Calais expedition appear disproportionate.[2]

When the pandemic of bubonic plague that swept westwards out of Asia across the whole of Europe reached England in 1348, Ilfracombe must have suffered like every other town and village—but it is no more possible to judge how many of its inhabitants died than it usually is elsewhere. All that can be said is that, whereas in some places mortality among the clergy during the second half of the 14th century tended to be high (after the first outbreak had burned itself out, plague recurred three times at roughly ten-year intervals) in Ilfracombe this was not the case. Although John de Lestre, who had been instituted in 1335, was indeed succeeded by a new incumbent, William Besta, in March 1348, de Lestre can hardly have died from plague, since the infection did not reach the shores of England until the summer. Besta's immediate successors were William Polgrim, 1361-c. 1382, and Thomas Barton, whose will was proved in 1416. However, this is negative evidence, and may indicate no more than that Besta, Polgrim and Barton were rather less assiduous in tending sick parishioners than some of their brethren elsewhere.

After Thomas Barton, who became successively Prebendary of Crediton and of Exeter, came Hugh Herle, a descendant of a Margaret Polglas, who, on marrying Sir William Herle, had carried the Champernowne inheritance into that family. William Besta had been the last incumbent to be presented to the living by a Champernowne. Hugh Herle's date of death is not known, but in 1439 Bishop Lacy licensed Master John Morton to perform divine service in the parish church, its three dependent chapels, and the chapel of the patron, which was in the house built by the Champernownes, known as Champernownewyke.

Evidence that Morton's probity was rather less than might be hoped of a parson is provided by contemporary chancery proceedings relating to West Country shipping. In 1433 two Cornish merchants petitioned the Bishop of Bath and Wells, chancellor of that court, to 'send a writ after John Mourton to appear before him in chancery on a day and under a penalty to be fixed by him to be examined'. Their case was that they had delivered certain merchandise to their attorney, Hugh Michelstowe, to take from Cornwall to Ireland to trade. When Michelstowe arrived in Waterford, 'John Mourton, clerk, parson of the church of Ilfracombe in Devonshire, had come to him and told him that he had lately been taken at sea by the king's enemies and put to ransom for a great sum and set on land in a strange country where he had no friends. He begged Hugh Michelstowe to help him with £40 in money to pay his ransom, and the latter, seeing that he was in great distress, agreed to help him provided that he would be bound in an obligation of £40 to him and to John Skyle, master of the ship that Hugh was in'.

The rector agreed, and himself wrote out his promise to pay the sum of £40 to Michelstowe and Skyle within ten days of the arrival in England of his servant, William Lyttleton. Evidently Skyle knew nothing of this agreement, since Morton was able to go to him secretly and persuade him to make a general release with the intention of barring Hugh Michelstowe from an action at law, in return for 40s. cash.

Unfortunately the outcome of this case does not appear. Morton, his mysterious voyaging on the high seas long past, died in 1459, leaving £2 13s. 4d. to be divided between 'sixteen of the poorest women of his parish in childbed', and desiring that two of his books, *Aurea Legenda* and *Pupilla Oculi*, might be chained within the chancel of the Ilfracombe parish church 'for ever'.[3] Like so many of those optimistic 'for evers' in medieval documents, this one was probably of fairly short duration; at the latest, the books would have been destroyed in the 17th century by Cromwell's followers.

Medieval ship owners and merchants had to put up with bureaucratic constraints in addition to their perennial anxieties about bad weather and piracy. Henry Vaghan, a merchant of Bristol, petitioned the chancery court in 1463 for the release of a consignment of Welsh frieze and other cloth which he had recently shipped 'by virtue of the king's licence under the great seal' aboard a Spanish ship of 100 tons, the *Mary of Guipuscoa*. He had 'fully paid the king's officers all the customs and tolls due on the cloth, as the cocket, paid and delivered under the seal of the Bristol customs, showed'. After sailing from Bristol, the ship was driven into Ilfracombe by contrary winds, as ships so often were; whereupon she and her cargo were seized by Lord Fitzwarren and his officers and detained. William Bourchier, Lord Fitzwarren, holder of the barony of Barnstaple, was at that time employed on commissions concerning shipping in the West Country. It seems that Vaghan's licence to trade abroad may have been out of date, thus justifying the arrest, but not surprisingly he felt himself greatly aggrieved, and begged the chancellor to address a writ to Fitzwarren 'strictly ordering the delivery of the cloths to the petitioner or his attorney, in accordance with faith and conscience, and he would pray heartily to God for him'.[4]

Attacks on foreign ships without any vestige of a lawful reason were probably frequent. For instance, in 1483 a French ship chartered by merchants of Bridgwater to bring a cargo of wine from Lisbon was plundered by an Ilfracombe vessel, and in the same year pirates from Wales swept down on another French ship when she had come in under the shelter of Hillsborough.

By this time Ilfracombe had been for a century subject to the port of Exeter, and no longer possessed whatever semblance of comfortable independence

had caused Plantagenet kings to make exorbitant-sounding demands on her.
The Norman manor of the Champernownes was now in the possession of Cecily,
Marchioness of Dorset, Lady Harington and Bonville. She was the only child of
the sixth and last Lord Harington, who was killed at the battle of Wakefield in
1460, when she was a baby. As a very young girl she married—or, rather, was
married to—Sir Thomas Grey, first Marquis of Dorset, by whom she had 15 children (George Grey, presented by her to the living of Ilfracombe in March 1524,
would have been a relation). Her grandson Sir Thomas Wyatt was created Duke of
Suffolk, but like his unfortunate daughter, Lady Jane Grey, he was executed by
Mary Stuart, and his estates forfeited to the crown. These must have been considerable, as his grandmother, the Marchioness, had had large properties in Devon,
Cornwall, Dorset, Somerset, and Wiltshire. Her surveyor, Richard Phellyps, took
a complete survey of them in 1525. In Ilfracombe she had about 35 principal
tenants, although because much of the property was held on the old system of a
term of three lives, the names of a man's wife and one child often appear in
addition to his own. The Torrs, for instance—then divided into four parts totalling
110 acres—were held by Robert Arkenoll, Wilmot, his wife, and Thomas, their
son, 'for the term of their lives according to the customs of the manor' for a
yearly rent of £2 6s. 8d. The survey shows that Lord Fitzwarren had recently
built a new mill; the water course running to it 'used to yield £5 6s. 8d., but now
is granted with the water course of Helemyle (Hele Mill) to Thomas Nicholl and
Robert Ware for the term of their lives for a rent of £4 13s. 4d.'; a welcome rent
reduction, no doubt. Another item records, however, that 'The miller of the mill
of Heyle', by which Hele is presumably again intended, 'for the lady's water'
paid only one shilling a year. Chambercombe itself was rented by a Thomas Dyer,
who farmed 152 acres there, and another 30 in two smallholdings elsewhere in
the parish.

The names of several of these leaseholders appear also in a subsidy roll of
almost the same date as the survey, although as was often the case, spellings
tend to differ: Richard Sterry on the subsidy roll becomes Richard Sturry on the
survey; William Makeschow becomes William Maxschyll; and John Cornysch
becomes John Cornysshe. But it is this list of taxpayers that makes it clear that in
comparison with Barnstaple, in particular, the people of Ilfracombe were by no
means affluent. This subsidy was not assessed, like that of the 14th century, on
movable goods only, but on wages, goods or land. Goods, on which all but three
of the town's taxpayers were assessed in 1524-5, might include coin, plate, stock
of merchandise, harvested corn and household chattels, and evidently no one in
Ilfracombe owned a great deal of any of these things, judging by the small
amounts they had to pay; even the landowners—again one of them was a woman,
Joan Beare—must have had modest holdings. The total raised from some 135
people was just over £11, whereas in Barnstaple 231 people paid roughly £38
in all.[5]

A muster roll of Elizabeth I's time tells a similar story. The mustering of the
'able men' (the men of every parish between the ages of 16 and 60 who were fit
to fight) with their arms and equipment, effectively began in Henry VIII's reign,

and amounted to the establishment of a kind of Tudor Home Guard against possible French invasion. Those who could afford it had to provide armour and weapons; here again the assessments were made on the basis of land or goods. A man who received an income of between five and ten pounds a year from land, for instance, had to provide one *almain rivet,* a bow, a sheaf of arrows, a steel cap and a bill. An *almain* (German) *rivet* was a kind of light body armour consisting of a breastplate with an apron made of overlapping pieces attached by rivets and sliding in slots, and a 'bill' was much the same as an agricultural billhook, but mounted on a six-foot shaft. Even those too poor to be assessed individually ('those not charged according to the Statute') had to contribute towards the cost of a stipulated quantity of armour and arms: in the case of Ilfracombe this was two corslets (body armour worn by pikemen), two pikes, two calivers, and two murrions (calivers and murrions were small guns).

4.   A view of Hillsborough rising above the harbour entrance, with the ancient Warp House at the eastern tip of Lantern Hill. This engraving probably dates from about 1835.

In each parish 'presenters' were appointed who, having been duly sworn in, made returns according to the financial status of their fellow villagers or townsmen, adding the names of all 'able men'. The small numbers of able men listed, in relation to the probably population, in Ilfracombe, and indeed, all the parishes of north Devon, suggests that many managed to claim exemption in some way. In 1569, in the whole of the Hundreds of Braunton and Hartland, for instance, only 833 able men were recorded.

Ilfracombe's presenters returned 51 in all—13 archers, 14 harquebusiers, 14 pikemen, and 10 billmen. (A harquebus was an early type of firearm, about three feet long and weighing some ten pounds, fired, no doubt very hazardously, by igniting gunpowder in a pan with a lighted wick.) There was only one man in the town in the five to ten pounds a year land-owning class, one who owned goods to the value of between £20 and £40, and five who owned goods valued at between £10 and £20. This compares poorly with the other towns, and even some of the larger villages, of the area.[6]

5. In this engraving of about 1850, by W. Willis, the Warp House is unaccountably not shown.

In its ownership of shipping, too, Ilfracombe was inferior to other ports in the north of Devon. All through Tudor times she probably had few merchant ships, and those very small. When Thomas Colshill, surveyor of customs for the port of London, compiled his register of trading vessels in 1572, he reported just three for Ilfracombe: the *Mary Fortune* of 30 tons burden, the *George* of 16 tons, and the *Jhon* (*sic*) of 10 tons. Bideford had six, the largest of 80 tons, while Barnstaple had 12, and there, too, the largest was of 80 tons. Evidence from port books, first introduced at the beginning of Elizabeth's reign, shows that between Ilfracombe and the ports of South Wales—Tenby, Milford Haven, Cardiff—in the last decades of the 16th century, sailed tiny coasters of as little as six or seven tons burden, carrying 'fardels' or packs of linen and 'frises' (the coarse wool cloth, frieze, then much used for everyday wear by working people), 'ballets' of canvas, raw wool, iron, brass, soap, cheese, sugar, 'pieces' of raisins, barley, and occasionally wheat or wine. Their names were Gallicised: there were *La Juliane de Ilfarcombe* of six tons, and also *Le Julien de Ilfarcombe* of eight tons; there were *La Cateren de Ilfarcombe* of 10 tons, and *Le Jehsus de Ilfarcombe* of 12 tons.[7]

As has already been mentioned, when English monarchs were sending armies into Ireland, Ilfracombe was one of the ports used for embarkation. Soldiers were usually directed to assemble at Barnstaple, but it seems that on occasions they then marched north to the coast. In 1558 the Privy Council sent a long letter of reproof because a contingent of 100 men had apparently been left kicking their heels in the town for several weeks while Sir Thomas Dennis, Sir John St Leger and Sir John Chichester were waiting to be informed as to what to do with them. In 1579, orders were given for 'provisions of victual for 600 men' to be embarked at Barnstaple on 30 July, but on 4 September 'the soldiers from Barnstaple met off Ilfracombe on their passage for Ireland'. Ten days later they had crossed the sea and were moving towards camp at Kilnagour. In 1585 Ilfracombe itself was ordered to provide victuals as well as shipping for an even larger draught of soldiers: 800 of them this time, which must have been a considerable strain on the town's resources.

Dramatic and, as it must have seemed at the time, unhappy news of Drake's round the world voyage of 1577–80 reached Ilfracombe in June 1579. Captain John Winter, commanding the *Elizabeth* of 80 tons, one of Drake's tiny squadron, had become separated from his companions in the Strait of Magellan during a tremendous storm. According to one account in Hakluyt, he virtually cut and ran against the wishes of his crew; according to another, he intended to search for Drake, but his crew over-ruled him. However it was, he sailed into Ilfracombe harbour, bringing with him a quantity of the medicinal bark of a certain South American tree, known for centuries as Winter's Bark and later given the botanical name *Drimys Winteri*. He had dosed his sailors with it as an anti-scorbutic. From the moment the *Elizabeth* dropped anchor under Lantern Hill, rumours of all kinds must have spread out across north Devon.[8]

The small size of Ilfracombe's ships may well have precluded their owners from applying for letters of marque, which were virtually permission to sail on voyages of piracy against Spanish vessels. But Barnstaple ship-masters sometimes brought prizes into the port—perhaps because bad weather prevented their sailing on into Barnstaple Bay and crossing the Taw's dangerous bar. In 1591, Philip Wyatt, Barnstaple's Elizabethan town clerk and diarist, recorded on 12 October that 'a bark of this towne which had been a reprising called the *White Hart* put into Ilfordcombe brought home some elifants teth' (i.e., tusks). Two years later he noted briefly that the *White Hart* had been taken—presumably by a Spanish ship—but that 'The *Gifte* a reprisal ship of this towne belonging to W. Morcomb and others carried a rich price (*sic*) into Ilfordcombe'.

An influential merchant of Barnstaple, John Delbridge, owner of yet another reprisal ship, made it his business to gather news of Spanish plans and activities from his agents abroad, and pass them on to Secretary Cecil. In September 1602, he reported that 'last night a bark from Ireland arrived at Ilfracombe reporting a landing of Spaniards in Ireland'. He enclosed a report from John Clemott, of Swansea, who had just come from Waterford, that 'three weeks ago 1,500 Spaniards landed in the west at Limerick, and that a greater number are expected. The Lord President was to come to Waterford, and all the gates to be made fast but one. I know not what fight there was at their landing'.

There seems some confusion in this report. It had been in September 1601 that a force of some 4,000 Spaniards under Juan de Aguila had landed at Kinsale in an attempt to help Hugh O'Neill to drive the English out of Ireland. They had been defeated by Charles Blount, Lord Mountjoy; Aguila had made terms and withdrawn to Spain. Either John Clemott had passed on a new scaremongering rumour a year after Aguila's landing, or Delbridge's letter had been wrongly dated in the relevant Calendar of State Papers.

Chapter Three

PARSONS AND PARISHIONERS, *c.*1550–1650

WHILE, IN TUDOR TIMES, a growing spirit of enquiry and adventure sent more and more men out across the oceans, a domestic version of that same spirit caused others to explore their own country with a new sense of excited discovery. They prepared maps; they provided information on the best way to travel; they noted what was worth seeing in this place and that. As early as 1544 a printer in Fleet Street brought out what he called *A Chronicle of Yeres,* which included such facts as 'the lengthe, bredth and compasse of Englande; with the number of parysche churches, townes, byschoprykes, and chyres in the same; besydes Cyties, and Castels. And also the wayes leadynge to the most notable places, and the distaunce betwyxte the same'. Christopher Saxton, a brilliant topographical draughtsman, began to survey and draw careful maps of every county in England and Wales, with the authority of the queen, in about 1574. His map of Devon, beautifully engraved in colour by Remigius Hogenberg of Mechlin, marks seven place-names along the northern coastline. Just one, Lynton, is spelled as we spell it today. The others, from east to west, are Cunisbere (Countisbury), Trensow (Trentishoe), Berye Arber (Berrynarbor), Combemerton (shown as some distance from the sea), Ilfarcombe and Mort. Off Morte skim three small ships, like mayflies, each with a single sail spread: an impression, perhaps, of those tiny coasters that carried their eight- or ten-ton cargoes up and down the Bristol Channel.

When John Leland, Henry VIII's librarian, presented the king with the manuscript of his 'laboriose journey and serche for Englandes antiquities' as a New Year present in 1546, he explained that he had been 'totally inflammid with a love to see thoroughly al those partes of this your opulent and ample reaulme'. Regrettably, he ignored the whole line of the coast from Countisbury to Morte, turning inland just beyond Minehead to cross Exmoor by way of Simonsbath, visit Barnstaple, Bideford and Torrington, and travel on into Cornwall. But William Camden, writing his *Britannia* 40 years later (and relying heavily on Leland's work in the process, according to contemporary critics) did at least acknowledge the existence of Ilfracombe; having devoted some space to Barnstaple, and discussed the difficulty of identifying Kenwith Castle, he added: 'After this, nothing there is to bee seene upon this coast but Ilfarcomb, a good and sure rode for ships, and Comb Marton bordering hard upon it'.

Camden brought out the first edition of his *Britannia* in 1586, in Latin; he was then thirty-five. There seems to be no record of his earlier journeys in search of

17

material for his book, but in June 1588, according to Anthony Wood's *Athenae Oxoniensis,* 'he took a journey (Oxford being in his way) to Ilfarcomb in Devonshire, in order to obtain more knowledge in the Antiquities of that Country (*sic*) and elfewhere, for the next Edition of his *Britannia,* and on the 6th February following he was made Prebendary of Ilfarcomb in the Church of Salisbury in the place of one J. Holman; which Prebendfhip he kept to the time of his Death, and then Edward Davenant succeeded him. The faid Journey, and others that he took for that purpose, the expenfes of them were defrayed by Dr. Gabriel Goodman'. Since Camden was, and remained all his life, a layman, this presentation appears as an example of the remarkable way in which benefices might be distributed, in those days, as a mark of personal favour.

Oliver, in his *Ecclesiastical Antiquities* of 1840, quotes Wood, as well as Lysons' statement that there was a tradition that Camden stayed in Ilfracombe, but adds that he has looked in vain for any authority for this. However, the *Dictionary of National Biography* observes that 'according to tradition Camden resided in the ancient vicarage, which he in part rebuilt. After a more extensive reconstruction *c.* 1750, his coat of arms remained to be seen in a room that had been turned into a kitchen until 1888, when the parsonage was demolished and a new one built on the site'.

The first incumbent of Ilfracombe to become a prebendary of Salisbury Cathedral had been Henry VIII's chaplain, George Carew, one of the two notable pluralists whom the king personally presented to the living, which was then worth £50 4s. 3d. a year. The other was Thomas Brerwode, Doctor of Degrees, who was rector of Bradninch, vicar of Colyton, rector of St Ewe, prebendary of Crediton, Exeter and Probus in Cornwall. Yet he was far outdone in this multiple holding of livings by Carew, who, Oliver says, 'held a Canonry in Exeter Cathedral, was Archdeacon of Totnes, became Precentor of Exeter, was Archeacon of Exeter, which office he resigned in 1569 for a pension of £20, and got the Deanery of Exeter in 1570, which he held to his death in 1583. In 1535 he was in actual possession of a Canonry in Crediton Church, the Free Chapel of Otter Mohun, the Vicarage in Brixham, the Rectory of Stoke Flemyng, the Rectory of East Allington, and the Rectory of Lydford, and subsequently he obtained the Deaneries of Bristol, of Christ Church, Oxford, and of Windsor, and the Precentorship of Salisbury'. One may wonder whether Ilfracombe ever actually received any pastoral care at all from these richly-endowed clerics.

Carew became, in his turn, patron of the living, to which he instituted Geoffrey Clepit in 1555. 'This is the first mention of the Prebend of Ilfracombe, which was constituted in exchange for Beer and Charminster by an Act of Parliament in the 37th year of Henry VIII (1546). Thus the incumbent of Ilfracombe was henceforth no longer Rector but Vicar, and the great tithes went to Salisbury'.[1]

It was during Geoffrey Clepit's incumbency that Ilfracombe, at last, began to keep parish registers. Thomas Cromwell, Henry VIII's lord privy seal and Vicar General, had ordered the keeping of such registers in 1538, but the first volume surviving of 'The Register booke of the Parishe Churche of Ilfardcombe, wherein is written Christnings, weddings and burieings' (as it was headed) dates from 1567.

It was copied out in 1602 by George Milton, who described himself as a scrivener when entering, in February of that year, the burial of the wife he had married only 18 months earlier. It is just possible that there was an earlier volume covering the years 1538 to 1566 which was lost, but it seems more likely that during the period when Ilfracombe was nominally in the care of Thomas Brerwode and George Carew, church matters in the parish were neglected, and that Clepit for a number of years was content not to concern himself with the keeping of records.

The surnames of those baptised, married or buried during 1567 include many that were still to be found in the town for several centuries afterwards: Atkey, Cornish, Periman, Eastaway, Davy, Dyer, Dennis, Ball, Netherway, Skinner, Quinte, Snow, Warren. There were no unusual Christian names for either boys or girls in this first year: we find Joan, Alice, Ellen, Elizabeth, Lucy, and John, Henry, Philip, Peter, Thomas, and David. But later, parents occasionally chose such names as Pernel, Mellis, Wylmot, Gyllian, Oringe, Ulalia, and Richaurde or Richord for their daughters, and Archelaus, Hanniball, Achillis and such biblical names as Zachariah, Melchizedeck, Shem, Obadiah and Nathan for their sons.

In the first 100 years of the registers the annual number of baptisms varied from as few as 18 in 1595 to as many as 56 in 1644; there were usually about 25 to thirty-five. Similarly burials might be as few as 11 or as many as 59, with the total ordinarily lying between 16 and thirty. Thomas Wainwright, who transcribed the copy of the registers preserved in the North Devon Athenaeum, Barnstaple, estimated that for this period there was a stationary population of about 1,000 to 1,100 in the parish.

At times weddings were rare events: several years between 1572 and 1653 show no more than three, though the number might rise to 17 and occasionally eighteen. The old rules of the church prohibiting marriage at certain times of the year were still in force in Elizabeth's reign; they were expressed in the rhyme:

> Advent marriage doth deny,
> But Hilary gives thee liberty,
> Septuagesima says thee nay,
> Eight days from Easter says you may.
> Rogation bids thee to refrain
> But Trinity sets thee free again.

An Act was passed during the Commonwealth period, in 1653, decreeing that banns of marriage should be published 'on three successive Lord's days, at the close of the morning exercise in the public meeting place commonly called the Church, or the Chapel, or in the market place next to the said Church or Chapel, on three market days in three several weeks next following, between the hours of 11 and 2', and that those intending to be married should come before some Justice of the Peace and without any religious observances, after a simple declaration that they took each other as husband and wife, and a promise on the man's part to be loving and faithful—and on the woman's part to be loving, faithful *and* obedient—they were to be declared by the Justice to be man and wife.

For Ilfracombe couples, this meant travelling to Barnstaple; no Justice of the Peace was available in their own town. The first marriage contracted under the new Act took place on 22 September 1654, before one of the Barnstaple borough magistrates, Thomas Matthews. In the next few years more than 50 couples made the journey to Barnstaple (one went as far as Torrington) for a civil marriage. By 1659, however, although the Act had not been repealed, people evidently felt that it was safe to ignore it, and began to go to church to be married once again.

As far as the registers of burials were concerned, it was a long time before anything but name and date was entered (although if a woman was a widow the fact was noted), but from the mid–17th century some sort of descriptive detail was occasionally added, especially if the cause of death was drowning. In October 1653, for instance, 'part of a shipps companie called ye *John* were drowned at our harbour's mouth'. Seven Englishmen and two Frenchmen were lost in this wreck, and a tenth man 'died in our town'. Four years later Nicholas Smyth was drowned 'within the Kaie he came into the harbour in a small barque that did belong to Newfoundland'. No doubt the small barque was engaged, like so many ships from Devon ports, including possibly Ilfracombe, in the Newfoundland fishing trade.

Quite often an entry shows that a man or woman who died was 'a stranger' and that he or she came from Wales, or Ireland, or somewhere nearer—Braunton, Northam, Bideford. If the person was of some wealth or local consequence, that too was noted: one mercer and two shipwrights appear in the 17th century, as do several vicars and their wives. One parson in particular evidently gained the special regard of his parishioners: when John Reade, who had been instituted in 1636, died in 1650, three years after his wife, Jane, the register recorded that he had been 'minister of the gospel of Jesus Christ and a faithful and precious pastor'.[2]

It is possible that John Reade had made a pleasant contrast to his immediate predecessor, Robert Liverland, who resigned after only three years. A terrier (a description of land holdings) made in about 1633, the year Liverland was instituted, suggests that he was dissatisfied with the amount of tithes paid; was he, in consequence, a neglectful vicar?

'A Terrier of the glebe lands and tithes belonging to the prebend of Ilfercomb', the document begins, and proceeds to detail them: the Church Park, a field of three acres running down to the West Wilder Brook; the tithing close of four acres, to the south of the Church Park; the Broad Park (a name that survives today) of nine acres; the Lamb Park and the Kerne—the old name for the Cairn— and a close called the Kerne's Close. There were also two small closes near the church and six tenements, each consisting of 'a house and backside' and bringing in one pound a year.

The terrier goes on to speak of 'the grounds which Mr. Dodridge has taken away from me . . . always formerly rented by the Vicar at £4 8s per ann. which is well worth £9 per ann.' and ends 'This is a good and large parish, and the tithes cannot be less than £200 yearly, so that the Tenants paying but £50 for the old rent and no taxes or charges, they have full £200 above the rent'. The peevish

6. A painting dated 1805 showing Ilfracombe still a compact little town clustering around the harbour and climbing the slope towards the parish church. The banner-flaunting fort on the hilltop to the left is evidently the 'castle' of Civil War times and earlier which is still commemorated in street names.

tone of these remarks suggests that Robert Liverland soon began to look about for a richer living.

To return to the parish registers: in the days of the Commonwealth, funeral services, as well as marriage services, were dispensed with, though a fee was charged for registering a burial. Some widowers evidently balked at paying this fee. When Susan, the wife of William Snowe of Watermouth, was buried on 15 September 1658, the register bore the bitter note 'He loved his wife soe well as not to pay for the registring of her name', and similar remarks appear against several other names in that year.

One of the most often quoted entries concerns the burial, in August 1644, of 10 men and one woman 'slain in ye fight ye 20th day'. Like Barnstaple and other towns of north Devon, Ilfracombe supported the Parliamentarians, and these deaths resulted from an attempt by Sir Francis Doddington to seize the town. According to the *Kingdom's Weekly Intelligencer* for 3 September 1644, 'at a town called Ilfordcombe in Devonshire, that Saint-like Cavalier Sir Dorrington (*sic*) set that town on fire, burnt 27 houses in the town, but was beaten out by the townsmen and sailors, and lost many of his men'. (Traditionally, the worst fighting took place at a field at the junction of the East and West Wilder brooks—now built over—which was long known as Bloody Meadow.

R. W. Cotton observes that although Ilfracombe lay outside the area of actual contest 'it seems that the town had quietly been put in some way of defence. It possessed a fort, the name of which, Ilfracombe Castle, indicates that it had been built in Tudor times, for the protection of the harbour and its shipping, when Dunkirkers, Biscayan and Algerine pirates haunted the entrance of the Bristol Channel. (Even in 1625, according to a letter sent by the Mayor and aldermen of Bristol to the Privy Council, three so-called Turkish pirates had taken Lundy 'with the inhabitants', and had threatened to burn Ilfracombe.) The situation of this work cannot with any certainty now be determined, but it is probable that it occupied the site of the present Quayfield House and grounds, on the steep acclivity which rises above the harbour[3] . . . The road from Exmoor through Combemartin by which it may certainly be conjectured that Doddington approached Ilfracombe, passed under the walls of the castle, on its landward side, before entering the town'.[4]

Although Doddington retired after his unsuccessful attack, within three weeks Ilfracombe had fallen, apparently because its governor had Cavalier sympathies. His name is not recorded, but when his counterpart in Barnstaple sent to him for gunpowder, he turned his guns on the deputation, and the next day surrendered to General Goring's troops, handing over 20 pieces of ordnance and 200 arms, as well as a quantity of gunpowder.

Presumably Ilfracombe Castle, or fort, was then occupied by a small Royalist garrison until in 1656 it was stormed by the Parliamentary Colonel Sheffield. In the *Moderate Intelligencer* for 11 April it was reported that 'Ilfracombe Fort is yielded, it commands a brave harbour; it was well manned and victualled: we shall now prevent any from landing and relieving any, by the help of the harbour'.

Chapter Four

THE HARBOUR AND ITS TRADE 1650–1800

ALTHOUGH in 1642, 1644 and 1647 the death rate in Ilfracombe rose to nearly twice the yearly average, the town did not suffer as severely from outbreaks of sickness as did many other places during the Civil War. Once the war was over, Ilfracombe's troubles were the practical ones of trying to earn a living from mainly coastwise trade, when every ship that went to sea was in frequent danger of attack by foreign vessels. In 1656 Ilfracombe joined with Barnstaple, Bideford and Minehead to petition the Privy Council for two 'small nimble frigates' to be stationed, one at Kinsale on the southern coast of Ireland and the other at Ilfracombe itself, to convoy and protect the traders sailing between the two ports carrying cargoes of wool, corn, tallow and cattle. (The latter, in the tiny wooden ships, must often have endured hideous discomforts, but it was a trade that was to continue for centuries: Lilian Wilson, in *Ilfracombe's Yesterdays,* quotes a Mrs. Buckingham, born in 1838 and still alive in 1932, who could remember Irish cattle being landed; local men helped to unload the animals 'hoisting them up with block and tackle, then throwing them overboard to swim ashore'. On these occasions, people living in the harbour area put up their shutters and bolted their doors 'as many of the animals were wild and savage'. After the treatment they had endured, it would have been surprising if they had been anything else.)

In the second half of the 17th century, Ilfracombe was still a sub-port of Exeter, with its boundaries fixed as Glenthorne to the east and Morte Stone to the west. It had its own Custom House (when Nathanial Handcock died in June 1670, it was noted in the register of burials that he had been 'collector of his Majesty's customs'—one of the few occasions in that period when a man's occupation was regarded as of sufficient importance to be recorded.) The port books for Ilfracombe show that in late Stuart times Ilfracombe was importing a good deal of coal, including the soft variety known as 'culm', from Tenby and Swansea. On the coquetts or cockets (documents warranting that goods had been duly customed) of the little coasters belonging to the port, such as the *Happy Return,* the *Pearle,* the *Catherine,* the *Neptune,* the *Safe Deliverance* and the *Speedwell,* the weight of coal is entered in 'chalders', that is to say chaldrons: eight, 11, 17, 20 chalders might make a ship-load. A chaldron equalled 36 bushels or 18 hundredweight, a kind of short ton.

When they were not carrying coals, the little ships might have a mixed cargo, including some of the unlucky cattle. In April 1686, for instance, the *Ann* of

Combe Martin ('Coomertin') sailed from Tenby carrying 13 cattle, 16 swine and one Welsh mare, as well as a quantity of wheat and malt, and in the same month the *Providence* brought nine score swine, 30 chaldrons of culm and 100 winchesters of barley. (A Winchester bushel or Winchester measure was a dry measure used in England from the time of Henry VII until 1836, when the imperial bushel replaced it.) The landing of 180 pigs in Ilfracombe harbour must have been a lively and noisy affair. The following month the *Happy Return* sailed into her home port from Bristol with an interesting assortment of goods, ranging from 'mesery' (mercery or silk goods and textiles) and haberdashery wares, paper, soap and glass, wheat and barley, hops and malt to wine, 'runletts of Strongwaters', brass, pewter and iron.[1]

The coasters usually had a crew of two—master and mate—just as their descendants in the 19th century, the West County trading ketches, usually did.[2] No doubt sons often went to sea with their fathers, and learned their seamanship in that way, but an orphan boy might be formally apprenticed by the parish to a master who agreed to 'teach and instruct and bring up, or cause to be taught and instructed and brought up . . . his said Apprentice in the trade or profession of a Mariner or Seafaring man which he himself now useth in the best way or manner that he may or can doe or devise to be done'. This was the form of agreement made by Lawrence Blinco of Ilfracombe when Marke Bowden was bound apprentice to him, for a term of six years, in 1691. Marke had to undertake to abide by all the usual restrictions of apprenticeship: not to play cards, dice or 'other unlawful games', not to frequent ale houses or taverns, not to marry or engage to marry, and not to absent himself 'from the service of his said Master neither by day nor by night'. In return, Lawrence Blinco promised to correct and chastise him only 'in a fair and gentle manner' and to provide 'competent and sufficient meat, drink, washing, lodging and apparel and all things fit and necessary for such an apprentice during the said term of his Apprenticeship'.

No doubt a number of Ilfracombe boys—though not necessarily orphans—were being apprenticed not only to seafaring, but to shipbuilding at this time. It may be surmised that at least some of the coasters entered as 'of Ilfracombe' (or simply 'of Combe', as they often were) had been built in the harbour, since, as has been said, it is reasonable to suppose that shipbuilding had gone on there for centuries. The occupation of shipwright is to be found in the parish registers in the second half of the 17th century: it appears against the names of John Cornishe, who was buried on 15 September 1654, and of John Norman, buried on 27 September 1695. Mortgage indentures held by Ilfracombe museum give us the names of several shipwrights—Walter Cope in Charles II's reign, and Humphrey Blackmore and William Vye in the time of the second and third Georges. (The name Vye was to remain of considerable importance in the town over the next century, members of the family being important property owners.)

Nevertheless, records of ships known definitely to have been built in Ilfracombe do not begin until 1735, with the brigantine *Edward* of 60 tons. Even then the name of the shipbuilder is not known. The *Edward* was followed, during the next 65 years, by another 60 vessels, although Grahame Farr suggests that there was never more than one principal yard, lying probably on the south side of the sheltered inner harbour formed by the old pier which, according to tradition, dates from the 14th century, and was first built by the Bourchiers.[3] Certainly it seems likely that it had been built before the mid-15th century, when William Bourchier, Lord Fitzwarren, was busy with commissions concerning West Country shipping.

The pier bears a commemorative tablet at its southern end; the inscription, surmounted by the Bourchier arms, begins:

> This extensive Pier, built some Ages since by the Munificence of the Bourchiers, Barons of Fitzwarine, Earls of Bath, and Vice Admirals of this Place, was in the year 1760 partly rebuilt, lengthened and enlarged by Sir Bourchier Wrey, Baronet, the present Lord and Inheritor of this Pier and Manor.

The reference to the Bourchiers as Vice Admirals is explained by the fact that Barnstaple district was created a separate vice-admiralty for the third Earl of Bath, who was Lord Lieutenant of Devon; according to Oppenheim, 'this temporary arrangement may have been the source of the impression that Barnstaple once possessed an Admiralty jurisdiction of its own'.[4]

In 1727, when the title of Earl of Bath had been for some time extinct, and their descendants the Wreys held the surviving manor of Ilfracombe (the Norman manor of the Champernownes having been dispersed in the 17th century) an Act for 'Repairing and Keeping in Repair the Pier and harbour of Ilfordcombe' was passed. This recognised that the harbour 'hath by long Experience been found to be of great Use and Benefit to the Western Parts of this Kingdom, and to all Seafaring Men, who by the Stress of Weather have been driven upon that Coast'. The quay or pier, the Act says, was 42 feet high and was 856 feet long 'or thereabouts'. (In fact, the stone pier itself can hardly have been more than about 300 feet, its present length, so the measurement quoted must have included the pier *and* the quay.) Not only the pier but the Warp-house at the harbour entrance, the lighthouse—in other words the light on the Chapel of St Nicholas—the pilot boats and the 'taw-boats' (towing boats) had all been 'at first founded and built and . . . constantly repaired and maintained at the private Expences of the Ancestors of Sir Bourchier Wrey'; however, the pier was now very much sunk and decayed 'by Length of Time and Violence of the Sea'; the Warp-house had long gone to decay, and the lighthouse and the boats for piloting and 'tawing' were very much out of repair 'to the great Prejudice of His Majesty's Revenue, and the Trade of the said Town of Ilfordcombe and parts adjacent'.

For this reason, the Act empowered Sir Bourchier to collect 'Sums, Duties and Acknowledgements'; for instance, a halfpenny a stone on all woollens and bay yarns and flocks, and eightpence a ton on goods of all other kinds. Ships seeking shelter in the harbour were to pay for the privilege (Michael Bouquet remarks that the south-westerlies that kept them storm-bound were known locally as 'Sir Bourchier's winds')[5] and from Michaelmas to the first of March all Ilfracombe ships were to pay sixpence towards the upkeep of the lighthouse; ships from

7. A late 18th-century painting by a local artist, Joseph Waters or Walters: 'An Exact Prospect of the Town and Harbour of Ilfracombe with a View of the Welsh Coast', taken from Hillsborough, shows shipping as it would have been at the time of the Napoleonic Wars. A privateer named the *Triumph* sailed from the port in those days, and her hulk was to be seen there at least as late as the 1890s.

elsewhere had to pay a shilling. The duty on tobacco was threepence a hogshead; for horses and bullocks the charge was a penny each; for sheep, fourpence for twenty.

In 1752 when Sir Bourchier Wrey, the sixth baronet (the Wreys kept the first name Bourchier for generation after generation) was M.P. for Barnstaple, he signed a document exempting the mayor and burgesses of that borough from all dues payable on their ships and merchandise entering Ilfracombe, 'in considera-tion of the especial regard and affection which I have and bear unto them . . . and for other divers good causes and considerations me thereunto especially moving'.[6] No doubt, during the previous 27 years, the merchants of Barnstaple had chafed against the provisions of the Act.

During the 18th century the number of vessels owned at Ilfracombe increased fourfold, from 15 to 60, and the total tonnage increased from 350 to 2,615, figures which do not include the smallest fishing boats and the craft of the hobblers, the boatmen who towed ships into harbour and serviced them. Some-what larger ships were occasionally being built in the shipyard; although the ordinary coaster did not exceed 60 tons, in the 1760s two of 100 tons were built, and in the 1780s there was one of 120 tons, the *Diligence,* and another, the *Diane,* of 200 tons. The *Diane,* in particular, was to be no local trader: she had an adventurous career carrying cargoes from London and Exeter to the Mediterranean and Spain, and later worked from Cornwall and south Devon, being boarded by a French privateer on one occasion, but escaping when the French captain's attention was distracted by another vessel.[7]

During this century Ilfracombe had a number of open boats engaged in fishing, principally for herring, but it was necessarily a fluctuating trade; in years when shoals deserted the western coasts, the people of a port such as Ilfracombe knew hardship.

The Revd. John Swete of Oxton House, Prebendary of Exeter, who visited Ilfracombe in 1789, said that there had recently been revived 'another article of commerce, which for forty years hath been unaccountably disus'd. I allude to the capture and seasoning of Herrings, which at periodical times are here taken in vast quantities, and being cured are afterwards exported to the Continent'. It was probably because an Act had been passed in 1786 to encourage British fishermen by paying them a bounty of a shilling a barrel that the revival had taken place. The herrings were cured in one of two ways, Mr. Swete explained: either 'in a common pickle of salt' or by salting and smoking. The latter method produced fish 'which from their colour are called Red Herrings'; these were counted into barrels holding about 900, 'of the number of which an oath is taken, a duty being exacted by Government'. The salted or white herrings were pressed as closely as possible into barrels holding from 1,200 to 1,400, and sold at from 15 to 24 shillings a barrel, whereas the red herrings might be worth as much as 50 shillings a barrel; evidently Continental buyers regarded the 'Combe smoked herring as a delicacy.[8]

Shipbuilding, it would seem, offered a steadier occupation than fishing. Between 1735 when the *Edward,* already mentioned, was built, and 1800, no fewer than 60 brigantines, sloops, schooners, smacks and skiffs were launched into the harbour: sturdy little wooden vessels of 14 to 80 tons, with just two, the *Prince George* and the *Arundel*, of as much as 100 tons. In traditional fashion, some were given the names of women—*Catherine, Betsey, Rebecca, Laura* and also *Loyal Betty* and *Charming Molly*—or of a woman and a man—*Thomas* and *Mary, George* and *Ann*; or they were called by optimistic and propitious abstract nouns or qualities—*Goodwill, Fortune, Diligence, Providence, Friendship, Fame, Concord.* Just a few derived from the natural world—*Sparrow, Swallow, Dolphin* and the poetic *Sea Flower.*[9]

It was shipbuilding on a very limited scale, with on average two small ships leaving the yard each year, but it must have given not only employment but an added sense of busy-ness to the life of the harbour. And only a few dozen yards away was the Rope Walk (still feebly remembered in 20th-century town plans as Ropery Road, a featureless alley behind the church of St Philip and St James) where men twisted hemp into cordage of all kinds to supply the shipyard and the needs of all mariners visiting or working about the quay.

Chapter Five

IN TIMES OF PERIL

FOR A CENTURY AND A HALF after the ending of the Civil War, Ilfracombe had only brief and more or less accidental involvement in national events. After the Battle of Sedgemoor, some of the Duke of Monmouth's followers, led by Colonel Nathaniel Wade, fled westwards. They seized a ship at Ilfracombe and set sail, but found that there were two frigates patrolling the north Devon coast. (It is not entirely impossible that the two 'nimble frigates' the town had asked for 30 years earlier were still on station.) Forced to land, the escapers separated. Colonel Wade managed to persuade a farmer's wife to give him food and find him shelter for a while in Brendon, but someone must have given him away. A letter containing a detailed account of his arrest was addressed to Sir Bourchier Wrey at Tawstock by Nicholas Cooke and Henry Ravening, 'apothecary and chirurgeon', who had been called in to tend the gunshot wound Wade had received while trying to slip away from the house in which he had been hiding. 'Ye bullett lodged in ye under part of ye right hypogastrind . . . right under ye pleura: from the orifice it entered to ye other, wch we were forced to make to extract the bullett . . . was in distance between six and seven inches . . . this day he was taken with a aguish fitt, which I suppose was caused by his hard diet and cold lodging ever since ye rout, he leaving his horse at Ilfordcombe'. (After what he had gone through, surgically, since being wounded, an aguish fit, one would suppose, would be the least of it.) The medical men on, 'We desire to know his Maties pleasure wt we shall due with his corps, if he dyes, wch if he does before ye answer, we think to embowell him. We will due wt possible we can, for he hath assured us, yt as soon as he is a little better, he will make a full discovery of all he knows, of wch this inclosed is part, by wch he hopes to have, but not by merrits, his pardon'.[1]

The letter was forwarded to the Earl of Sunderland, Principal Secretary of State. Wade recovered, and although he and his companions had been deeply implicated in the Rye House plot, they were allowed to live because, in Macaulay's words, 'they had it in their power to give information which enabled the King to slaughter and plunder some persons whom he hated'.

During the Seven Years War, a French 64-gun line-of-battle ship, the *Belliqueux*, was taken by H.M.S. *Antelope* off Ilfracombe; conceivably the sound of gunfire in the Bristol Channel took many townspeople up to the heights of Hillsborough or the Torrs to watch the capture.[2]

Later in the 18th century, reverberations of far-off British naval engagements against France reached the town in the form of two dramatic wrecks off Rapparee

Cove. The first was in 1782, when a French ship captured by Admiral Rodney off the West Indies—then an important naval base—was being brought back to England as a prize. She went on the rocks below Hillsborough. The second was in 1796; a pictorial record of it by a local artist exists and may be seen in the Ilfracombe museum: it bears the inscription 'Ilfracombe with a view of the bark *London* who came from St Lucia with 150 black prisoners and was wrecked in Rapparee Cove Oct. 9th, 1796'. The *London* was said to have been carrying French prisoners-of-war and British troops, in addition to the black prisoners, as well as a quantity of gold and silver. Traditionally, coins—and skulls and bones— were found on the beach from time to time, and it is a matter of record that in January 1978 a number of gold *escudos* were found by the owners of metal detectors. A correspondent writing to the *North Devon Journal* in February 1856, quotes an account of the wreck given in the *Annual Register* for 16 October 1796, which said that although the people of Ilfracombe did everything in their power to save passengers and crew, many were drowned, including some sixty of the West Indians imprisoned in the hold, 'and as they were washed in, not all at once, their bodies were buried deep in the sand'. Certainly the parish registers show no burials of 'strangers' at the relevant date.

The year before this wreck a sharp reminder of the continuing conflict with France had come to Ilfracombe. Owners of shipping were required to supply men for the Navy in proportion to the trade of their ports, and 49 were required from the town. And in 1797 the danger threatened to come into the harbour itself; in fact, many books have claimed that it was more than a threat—that French ships sailed in and scuttled several coasters, and that an Ilfracombe character named Betsy Gammon beat a drum round the town to rally other women, who then gathered on the hillsides with their red petticoats over their shoulders, thus giving the impression of redcoats waiting to repel invaders. To add credence to this spirited idea, the Ilfracombe museum displays Betsey's drum and a large segment of red flannel once the property of one Granny Scott. But as R. N. Worth observes in his *History of Devon,* 'there is hardly a seaport in Devon that has not some tradition of invaders being scared by a muster of old women in red cloaks'.

However, there is no doubt that at least three French ships did sail up the Bristol Channel in February 1797. In the diary of Philip Rogers Webber, Deputy Lieutenant of Devon, an entry appears for 22 February in that year: 'Ilfracombe alarmed by the report of a Pill pilot [presumably a pilot from the Avon Pill] that two French ships and a lugger had passed Lundy and were off 'Combe. The alarm was about midnight. By break of day no vessel was to be seen'.[3] The *Gentleman's Magazine* quotes from the *London Gazette* part of a letter written by Lieutenant-Colonel Orchard, commanding the North Devon Volunteers, to the Duke of Portland dated Heartland [*sic*] Abbey, 23 February 1797. In this Colonel Orchard reported that on the previous day he had received an 'express' from Ilfracombe mentioning that there were three French frigates off that place; that they had scuttled several merchantmen, and were attempting to destroy the shipping in the harbour. 'They begged that I would immediately order the North Devon Regiment

8. Another painting by Joseph Waters or Walters, made in 1796. It bears the inscription 'Ilfracombe with a view of the bark *London* who [sic] came from St. Lucia with 150 black prisoners and was wrecked in Rapparee Cove Oct. 9th, 1796'.

of Volunteers under my command to march to their assistance.' He duly gave the order, and was gratified by the men's prompt response, 'as diligent, orderly and sober as might be expected at a morning parade of an old regiment'. But before they could set off, he received another message from Ilfracombe: the French ships were gone from the coast and tranquillity was restored to the town. As a result, he thought it prudent to take the whole thing with a pinch of salt. 'How far the report was well founded I cannot possibly say, but, as this affair may be mis-represented and exaggerated, I trust your Grace will excuse my troubling you with this letter'.

Whether or not the French had done any damage in Ilfracombe harbour, and whatever cause they may have had to depart (if the alarm was raised at midnight, and there was no sign of them by the break of a February day, they could hardly have made out figures on the hillsides, however red their cloaks) they certainly sailed across to Wales and landed there—only to surrender almost immediately. The red cloak theme recurs on the north shores of the Bristol Channel: there, Lord Cawdor is said to have dressed his miners in their wives' red petticoats. With or without petticoats, the 'gentlemen and peasantry' showed 'great spirit and loyalty', according to a letter written to the Duke of Portland by Lord Milford; 'many thousands of the latter assembled, armed with scythes, and attacked the enemy, previous to the arrival of the troops'. Lord Cawdor himself reported that three large ships of war and a lugger having anchored in the road-stead at Haverfordwest, he had led a detachment of the Cardigan militia and all the provincial force he could muster to encounter the French, who seem to have been in an unbellicose mood. Their second-in-command presented him with a letter saying disarmingly (literally), 'The circumstances in which the body of French troops under my command were landed at this place render it unnecessary to attempt any military operations, as they would tend only to bloodshed and pillage'. Therefore, 'on principles of humanity', he surrendered himself and his 1,400 men.

This particular small episode of the Napoleonic War may have ended igno-miniously for the invaders, but knowledge of detailed French plans for attacks on Britain caused the Committee of Secrecy of the House of Commons, in 1799, to remind 'all Classes and Descriptions of His Majesty's faithful Subjects . . . to arrange themselves in arms . . . to repel a species of Invasion'. They knew, they said, of French intentions 'to raise a fresh and general insurrection in Ireland'. Local corps of volunteer infantry were therefore being raised: Robert Newton Incledon, the Deputy Lieutenant of Devon, issued a proclamation urging the inhabitants of north Devon to come forward in defence of their king and country and 'save themselves the disgrace and inconvenience of being compelled to do so':[4] a case of volunteer or else. Thus warned, after morning service one Sunday in August 1803, some 150 Ilfracombe men enrolled, many of them being sufficiently literate to sign their names, although a dozen or so had to make their mark. Nathaniel Vyc Lee was commissioned as captain.

According to White's *Directory* of 1878-9, a privateer named *Triumph* made Ilfracombe her home port during the Napoleonic Wars, and had a number of successes (though no doubt a considerably smaller vessel than the Navy's contemporary *Triumph*, a 74-gun line-of-battle ship). Her active life at an end, she became a hulk somewhere off Ilfracombe, and was still to be seen at the time the *Directory* was published.

Even when not directly affected by public events, the people of Ilfracombe did not ignore them: throughout the 18th century the churchwardens' accounts show payments to the ringers to celebrate all kinds of national occasions considered suitable for rejoicing, from the birth of a prince to the winning of a battle by land or sea, or better still, the signing of a peace treaty.

In Tudor times the parish church had five bells. These were broken up in 1716 and re-cast as a peal of six, which proceeded to ring out on a Thanksgiving Day appointed 'for the suppression of the rebellion in Scotland'. The rising of 1745 was similarly celebrated, as was the taking of 'Quebeck' in 1759 and naval victories during the Napoleonic Wars, such as Cape St Vincent and the Nile. More obscurely, there are such entries as 'To the Ringers at the news of the King of Sardinia's beating the French and Spanish in Italy' in 1746, and 'To the Ringers on Taking of Louisburg and the Defeat of the Russians' in 1758.

It is reasonable to suppose that a number of Ilfracombe men joined, or were pressed into, the Navy; but if their service was on the lower decks their identities remain as unknown as those of the 49 conscripts of 1795. However, the names of at least two families in the town, the Bowens and the Downs, are on record as having produced officers who served at sea in the Napoleonic Wars. Edward Down arrived in Ilfracombe as a preventive officer in the 1760s; in October 1767 he married an Ilfracombe girl, Mary Sommers, and one of their sons, also named Edward, joined the Navy at the age of 17 and was present at the battle of Ushant as a midshipman. By 1797 he was a master's mate; he was wounded at Cape St Vincent. At Trafalgar he commanded the *Adelphi*.[5]

Among the large family of Edward and Jane Bowen were three sons, James, Richard and George, who were all to see service in Nelson's time. The least distinguished, it seems, was George, born in December 1762, who retired to Torquay with the rank of captain and died in 1817. Richard, born in April 1761, was serving on H.M.S. *Foudroyant* in 1782.

Ten years later he took part in the attack on Martinique, and was promoted to command H.M.S. *Terpsichore,* a 32-gun frigate, which fought actions both in the West Indies and off the coasts of Spain. In Nelson's ill-fated attack by night on Santa Cruz, on Tenerife, in July 1979, he was in charge of one of the boats making up the landing party. It was as the result of a wound received at the moment of gaining the shore that Nelson lost his right arm. Captain Bowen— 'than whom', Nelson wrote, 'a more enterprising, able and gallant officer does not grace His Majesty's naval service'—was killed, as were several other officers and some 200 sailors and marines. A monument to him in white marble, surmounted by an ornate arrangement of maritime trophies and bearing a long inscription conventionally eulogising his virtues and courage 'erected by his afflicted Father', is to be seen in Ilfracombe parish church. According to the editor of Nelson's *Dispatches and Letters,* both Nelson and the Earl of St Vincent 'used great exertions to induce the Government to place a monument in his memory in Westminster Abbey', but without success.[6]

The third brother, James Bowen, was born in 1750, and first went to sea in the merchant service.[7] After commanding a ship in the African and West Indies trade, he entered the navy as a master, serving aboard H.M.S. *Artois* for eight years. He was appointed inspecting agent of transports in the Thames, but went to sea again at the request of Lord Howe as master of the flagship *Queen Charlotte*. Like Edward Down, he served at the battle of Ushant. Promotion then came rapidly: a lieutenant in June 1794, he became commander just a year later

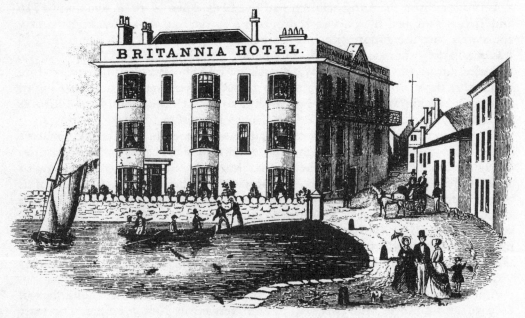

9.   The *Britannia Hotel*, built in the 18th century.

and captain after a further three months. Having commanded ships in the West Indies and the Mediterranean, he convoyed one of the East India Company's fleets to St Helena, and was presented with a piece of plate worth £400 for his 'care and attention' during this service. For superintending the re-embarkation of the British army at Corunna he received the thanks of both Houses of Parliament.

Having retired to Ilfracombe with the rank of rear-admiral, after spending the years from 1816 to 1825 as a commissioner of the navy, he evidently brought a considerable amount of property; his youngest son (who in spite of being christened St Vincent entered the church rather than the navy, and was curate of Holy Trinity, Ilfracombe) is shown by the 1839 tithe map to be one of the leading property owners. The admiral had six daughters, none of whom married, but lived all their lives in a house, Burrow Lodge (later Pembroke Lodge) built for them by their father.

To the ordinary people of Ilfracombe, in Stuart and Georgian times, the power struggles of the nations probably remained dramatic, but remote, events, affecting them directly only insofar as they added to the dangers of those whose livelihood came from the sea.

The population was slowly rising. It may have been about 1,100 in the mid-17th century;[8] Thomas Wainwright estimated that it had reached about 1,500 by 1766, and the first national census of 1801 showed that it was then 1,838. Although writers have tended to suggest that Ilfracombe remained a fairly poor place over the centuries, Defoe, on his tour of Great Britain in the 1720s, saw it as 'a good market and port town' and 'a town of good trade, populous and rich, all of which is owing to its having a very good harbour and road for ships'. He also observed that 'the merchants of Barnstaple do much of their business at the port of Ilfracombe' because of the age-old difficulty, in bad weather, of taking ships over Barnstaple Bar into the Taw-Torridge estuary. At about this time, Ilfracombe was sixth in order of importance among Devon ports in respect of foreign trade. Between Christmas 1714 and Christmas 1717, 29 ships of a total tonnage of 1,167 were cleared from her harbour. However, this is not a very impressive total: it amounts, after all, to less than 400 tons of merchandise a year, and apparently nearly half of it went no farther than Ireland.

For most of the 18th century, and in the early 19th, it was true to say that there were only two or three dozen people in Ilfracombe—a small number in proportion to the total population—too poor to support themselves.[9] Once or twice, in the 17th century, the words 'a poor man' appear against a name in the register of burials, and when a woman whose name is spelled 'fflourence' (no surname is given) was buried in January, 1637, the clerk identified her as 'one of the poore of the Church House'.

The Church House, here, as elsewhere, would have been built for various parish purposes: to house stores, to hold meetings of one kind or another, or to accommodate the revels known as Church Ales. It was in existence as early as 1525 when the churchwardens held 'one tenement called the Churchouse and pay yearly four pence'.[10] It is not known how soon its additional use as some kind of poor house began, but in February 1737, according to the heading of an account book of the churchwardens and overseers of the poor, 'The Church House was transformed into a Workhouse'.[11] The building stood at the top of the church steps. It was demolished over a century ago; at the end of its existence part of the upper storey was used as the girls' schoolroom of the Church School, while the ground floor, described by a contemporary writer as 'a long stable-like room', was still occupied by a few aged poor men.

In the first dozen years or so after the opening of the Workhouse there were not more than 20 inmates, often fewer; numbers rose gradually to over 40 in the late 1750s. (Additionally, small amounts of from 6d. to 1s. 9d. per week in poor relief were paid to some 130 individuals or families in the town, together with a number of 'extraordinaries' or casual payments.) The institution's accounts show the type of food, drink, clothing and general care offered to the inmates, the total cost of which was between three and four pounds a month at first, rising proportionately as numbers rose. Provisions included milk, potatoes, wheat, cabbage, cheese, groats, beer, occasionally beef or mutton, and herrings, bought by the barrel. Regular sums are entered for the cost of baking; it seems that the cook was a man, possibly one of the inmates. The Poorhouse (or the Poor's House, as it was often written) had its regular suppliers, each of whom signed a brief contract, 'I do agree to serve the Poorhouse with . . .' whatever it was, in the Vestry Minute Book.

The cost of food remained fairly constant over a period of 30 years or so. The price per pound of beef was from three halfpence to twopence farthing a pound, according to quality. Mutton was about the same, cheese a penny three farthings a pound, rice twopence halfpenny, butter threepence halfpenny, raisins three halfpence. Candles were comparatively expensive at fivepence a pound; tobacco was twopence halfpenny, and soap a penny three farthings. Beer cost three halfpence or twopence a gallon, wheat three shillings and eightpence a bushel (with a charge of fourpence for grinding), and potatoes one shilling and twopence a bushel.

If the poor people became ill, special items would be ordered for them: 'a bottle of wine for Elizabeth Bowen being sick'; 'milk for Goody Snow'; 'to raisins for Julian Lang in sickness'; 'to Joan Harris for a pint of wine and Cyder for John Berry in the Ague'; 'to a neck of veal for the sick'. Sugar was sometimes specially ordered; evidently it might be eaten ('to Sugar and Bread for Nathan Lang and Roger Hart in their Illness'), but it might be applied to the eyes ('to Gertrude Addams to buy white Sugar Candy for her Eyes'), with what effect it is hard to imagine. Often it seems that ale was give to 'those who tooke Physicke', either as a bribe, a consolation, or to wash down the nauseous medicine, brimstone and treacle, that was to continue to be administered, at least to children, into late Victorian times and beyond.

Regular medical attendance was provided. In May 1740 a Vestry Meeting agreed to elect 'an apothecary and a chirurgeon' for the Workhouse. 'Mr. Tawman and Mr. Clark hath agreed to take care of all the Persons now with the said Workhouse together with the Governour and Dame Joan in all that shall happen both in Physick and Chirurgory for the sum of £2'.[12] Among the medicaments ordered by Mr. Tawman were sassafras, melilot, yellow balsam, chamomile flowers, and spirits of wine; he prescribed stomachic and diuretic juleps, liniment, laxative boluses, and purging potions, and from time to time, less specifically, 'a paper of powders' or 'a bottle of drops'.

Mr. Clark's skills were called on to bleed unfortunate patients, and at least once he performed an amputation, removing the leg of one William Hughes 'and curing the same'. Another amputee received 'a wooden leg and knee', which cost seven shillings. And when inmates had gone beyond medical help, a shroud cost sixpence, the digging of a grave sixpence or a shilling, a coffin five shillings, and ale for the funeral a shilling.

Every now and then there was delivered at the Workhouse, quite literally, a load of old rope, almost certainly discarded from a local ship: one entry, for instance, reads 'Old rope from Captain Parminter, 2d.'. This was the raw material for the tedious task inflicted on workhouse inmates and prisoners alike, for centuries: picking oakum. The people of the Poor's House were expected to work at this and other tasks such as spinning, cleaning the church, repairing the walks in the churchyard and even sweeping the streets of the town. It does not seem that they were very eager to work; entries occur in the accounts of small sums given 'To the poor in the house for encouragement to do their labour'. The women who did the laundry were paid in tobacco; 'To tobacco for the Women at Washing' appears regularly.

The clothing supplied was of the coarsest: 'shifts' were made of canvas; hessian was bought for aprons and, perhaps, jackets; men wore hard-wearing serge breeches. By way of mattresses, 'bedsacks' of canvas were used. By the standards of the time, shoes were expensive: a pair for a man cost a penny more than a coffin, and for a woman as much as 26 lbs. of beef. Not surprisingly, they were carefully repaired; re-soling them was known as 'taping', and the little sprigs used to fasten the new soles were called 'sparables', i.e., sparrow-bills.

There were children in the Poor's House. Sometimes, it seems, they were taken to bathe in the sea, not perhaps very willingly: three-halfpence was paid 'To the Children when dip'd in Salt Water', and a Mrs. Martin was given ale 'for diping Mary Somers'. They also received some sort of education: horn books, a primer and a Child's Guide were ordered.

The first governor of the Poor's House was named Somers; the Mary Somers who was 'dip'd' was probably his daughter. Towards the end of the 18th century Governor Somers was replaced by John Dockett, who died in 1837 at the age of eighty-five. The Revd. Nesbitt includes in his history of Ilfracombe church the inscription on a gravestone near the lych gate to the memory of John Dockett and his wife, Mary; as he says, 'there is a delightful ambiguity about the concluding words':

> They was for many years Governor and Governess of the Poor's House near this Church of England all their days, and their mortal remains now Rest in those two graves in hopes of a joyfull Resurrection at the last day. What sort of people they was that day will discover.

Chapter Six

VARIETIES OF EDUCATION

THE FACT THAT HORN BOOKS and a primer were ordered for the children of the 'Poor's House' is a reminder that, for centuries before the Education Act of 1870, some degree of literacy was not necessarily confined to those whose parents could afford to buy them an education; from the early Middle Ages the Church had taught a number of poor scholars, and later, benevolent individuals endowed schools in their lifetime or through bequests.

It is not possible to know what facilities for learning were available in Ilfracombe before the 17th century, but one of the many facts to be obtained from the parish registers is that a school of some kind must have existed then. Against the name of Susanna, who was buried in December 1692, is entered 'wife of John Huxtable, schoolmaster', and when, seven years later, John Huxtable himself died, his profession is again noted in the register. Possibly things deteriorated after his death; certainly in 1729, according to Professor Hoskins, the only schoolmaster, who was also deputy controller of the port, and a boatman, had neglected his teaching duties for some 10 or 12 years.[1]

It may be that Gertrude Pincombe, 'a spinster of Welsbere in the parish of Poughill' had connections in Ilfracombe; the name Pincombe is to be found a number of times in the registers.[2] She left £10 a year in order that the churchwardens of 'Ilfordcombe' might pay six of them to a schoolmaster and four to a schoolmistress 'for teaching so many boys of the said parish, to be chosen by the minister, churchwardens and overseers, or the major part of them, as well such whose parents should have relief, as those whose parents should not have relief, the boys in reading English and arithmetic, the girls in reading English, and for instructing them in the principles of the church of England, till the boys should arrive at the age of 13 or 14, and the girls at the age of 12'.[3]

Nearly 100 years later the school was still in existence. In 1826 it was reported that a schoolmaster was teaching 12 boys and girls reading, writing and arithmetic 'on the Madras system'. This was the system evolved by Andrew Bell, who had been superintendent of an orphanage in Madras. In 1811, having returned to England, he was invited to set up what was known in full as the National Society for Promoting the Education of the Poor in Principles of the Established Church; the many schools established under his aegis were usually known as Bell's Schools or National Schools. His method involved setting long desks along the walls of a schoolroom, leaving the middle clear. Children doing written work sat at the

38

desks; reading or arithmetic groups stood in the cleared space . At the end of each lesson, the writers and readers changed places.

The yearly salaries of the Ilfracombe schoolmaster and schoolmistress had not increased in a century. By this time, there were 14 very young children being taught to read, and the girls were learning to knit and sew. The Pincombe Charity owned a considerable acreage of land, mostly at Hele and West Hagginton.

According to Lysons, there were 30 children maintained by voluntary contributions in 1822, a school of industry in which 44 girls were instructed, a Church of England Sunday school for 50 boys and 70 girls, and another for dissenters attended by 100 boys and 25 girls. In addition, as there existed in the town what one guide book called 'a respectable body of dissenters, Independents and Wesleyans' as well as a congregation of Plymouth Brethren, a daily school had recently been established 'on the principles of the British and Foreign School Society . . . which is held in the room attached to the Independent Chapel. In this School the Scriptures are taught, but no religious formularies are observed; the children of all denominations are readily received'.

When the Revd. John Mill Chanter (who was later to marry Charlotte, Charles Kingsley's sister) became vicar of Ilfracombe in 1836, the Church School was over the old Fishmarket 'which stood where the Clock Tower now stands, in the centre of the town. The Market was a quaint old place. You mounted a stairway outside the building to reach the school, the floors of which were uneven and rough . . . more fitted for a hay loft than a school. The school bell was from a ship, called the *Europa*, wrecked at Lee'.[4]

Private schools, presumably very small, were coming into existence. Pigot's *National Commercial Directory* of 1830 names four 'Academies or Schools'; two were listed as boarding and day schools, a third as a day school; concerning the fourth there were no details. In 1840 a Mr. Page, of Belvedere Place, advertised his 'Classical, Commercial and Mathematical Establishment'; he claimed to have had five years practical experience in land surveying and engineering. Mrs. Page gave lessons in 'the different styles of drawing in Pencil and Colour'; other accomplishments were taught by masters. About 30 young gentlemen had the opportunity to learn 'Greek, Latin, English and French Classics, Modern Geography, History, English Grammar and Composition, Mathematics, Bookkeeping and Commercial Accounts, the theory of Navigation, and the use of Globes'. For this comprehensive curriculum the fees were £30 a year (£36 with French, evidently a more expensive extra than Greek or Latin) for boarders, but only from £6 to £12 a year for day boys.

White's *Directory* of 1850 mentions three 'academies' in the High Street and one in Fore Street, but there is no record of the subjects they offered.

Possibly some of the boys who struggled with the classics at Mr. Page's establishment were expected by their parents to move on to public schools, while others studying navigation and the use of globes were destined for the navy. But a few who lacked the dubious advantage of being sent to fee-paying schools were offered the chance to learn Latin: the Revd. Chanter held classes at the vicarage for a number of boys and girls—presumably the more promising ones who attended the Church school—and Latin was among the subjects he taught, though only to boys. One of his pupils became a clergyman, another a schoolmaster; one of the girls remained to teach in the local school: 'with no other training [she] satisfied the Government Inspectors for nearly 40 years, keeping up the number of scholars and . . . gaining the love of the children, the respect of the parents, and satisfying the highest expectations of her old master'.

In his attitude to education, as in other respects, John Mill Chanter seems to have been exceptional among the incumbents of Ilfracombe. He held the living of Holy Trinity for 51 years, longer than any of his predecessors. Born at Hartland in 1808, he was educated at Blundells and Oriel College, Oxford, took his M.A. in 1834, and was ordained priest. A year or two earlier he had met the Kingsleys at Clovelly, where the Revd. Charles Kingsley, senior, father of the novelist, acted as curate for a year before being presented to the living by Sir James Hamlyn. When Mr. Kingsley left Clovelly in 1836 to become rector of Chelsea, he tried to persuade Mr. Chanter to go with him as his curate, without success: the opportunity to become vicar of Ilfracombe exerted a greater appeal.

Like John de Champernoun in 1333, and like Hugh Herle, who in 1416 complained that the rectory had been left in a sad state by his wealthy predecessor, Thomas Barton, John Chanter found himself occupying a dilapidated building, surrounded by equally dilapidated outbuildings, including a tithe barn and vicar's barn. The house itself had probably changed little since 1745; a terrier of that year describes it 'built with Stone Walls and covered with Slate Stones' containing 'five rooms on a Floor, two of which are of Deal, the rest of Lime Ashes, not wainscotted, but plaistered'.

The kitchen floor was still of limeash, with a surface like well polished marble, Chanter's daughter, Gratiana, recalled. In wet weather it would be an inch or two deep in water, 'so that the maids were obliged to trot about in pattens'. She describes it as a long low room with two deeply-latticed windows, a high mantelpiece, and huge oak beams 'clasped at intervals by richly carved bosses of the same wood'.

When rebuilding the south side of the vicarage at the time of his marriage to Charlotte Kingsley, the vicar preserved this ancient kitchen. However, when he retired in 1887, the Ecclesiastical Commissioners took the opportunity of demolishing the vicarage and building a new one on the site the following year; thus what is said to have been a part of the manor house of Camden's time was lost.

The church, in 1836, was in an even worse state than the vicarage, 'filled up with high worm-eaten pews' and containing five galleries, which darkened the interior. But what was worse was that the aisles had been taken up for interments, and the slabs put back again anyhow; a repulsive smell came from the old tombs. One peculiarity was that the chancel was considerably lower than the level of the nave, 'the builder having followed the slope of the ground, instead of taking the trouble to raise it, so that the Clergyman, when officiating, was quite lost to view by those sitting a little way back'. The windows were loose in wooden frames; they rattled and let in sharp draughts.

Chanter set about collecting money for restoration, and also for the building of the new church he considered necessary to cater for the town's increasing population. During the time that Dr. Pusey, one of the leaders of the Oxford Movement, was suspended from preaching in Oxford, he came to stay in Ilfracombe. The vicar invited him to preach. According to Frank Nesbitt, 'a great deal of excitement was caused in Ilfracombe by the fact that the man, whose name was, for those who did not know, the synonym of all that was bad, had been allowed to preach in the parish church'. Nevertheless, he evidently won over his hearers; his first sermon, in aid of the National Schools, raised £50, and the second, in aid of the new church, raised eighty pounds. When he returned the following year he attracted 'a crowded and deeply attentive congregation'.

Although Gratiana Chanter says that the restoration of Holy Trinity began in September 1860, Nesbitt quotes the *North Devon Journal* to show that replacement of the windows, at least, had begun by 1852. Work went on gradually, as funds permitted; the floors of the aisles were levelled and cemented, the chancel was raised, and, perhaps regrettably, the old pews and the galleries were taken out.

10. Holy Trinity Church, Ilfracombe, as it was in 1864, when the Rev. John Mill Chanter was vicar. (From Gadsby.)

In May 1851, Mr. Chanter laid the foundation stone of the new church, St Philip and St James. It was to be 1857 before it was completed 'and how many more years it might have taken, no one can say, had not a certain Mr. Stone come forward offering to finish it, with the understanding that after the first presentation it should be in his gift'.

The vicar, meanwhile, was continuing to raise money for new schools. Charles Kingsley preached on behalf of this fund. He was staying at Bideford in 1854, deep in the writing of *Westward Ho!*, and the Chanters were visiting Hartland; he travelled back to Ilfracombe with them, and took 'The Worthies of Devon' as the subject of his sermon. The church was crowded to hear him.

The funds raised over the years made possible the building, in 1863, of Holy Trinity National School for girls and infants, for 268 children; Holy Trinity Boys' School came 20 years later. A school for 220 pupils had already been built, in 1860, in association with St Philip and St James. Thus, well before the passing of the Education Act of 1870, a large number of Ilfracombe children had the opportunity of at least elementary education.[5]

It is almost certain that any organ that had been installed in the parish church before the Civil War was destroyed in 1644, when parliament issued an ordinance for the demolishing of 'all Monuments of Idolatry', which included 'all organs, and the frames and cases wherein they stand, in all Churches and Chapells'. In the 18th and early 19th centuries music was supplied by singers: in 1728, according to the Churchwardens' accounts, 'the two back Seats and the Pew shall be for the use and behoofe of those that are singers in the said Church', and in 1745 there was a payment for 'making a separation in the Singers' Pew in the Loft'. These singers may have been accompanied by stringed instruments; by the beginning of the 19th century their successors certainly were, as payments are recorded for strings for the 'Beas Vile', for violin strings and for a concert flute with four silver keys. The choir and choirmaster were paid. In 1810 the latter was a Thomas Pile, who received four guineas a year for 'teaching twelve young voices to assist the former Choir'. In 1825 a Mr. Wildman was receiving £4 for instructing the singers. The younger members of the choir, little girls in white tippets and caps, sat in an upper gallery (the loft already mentioned) and the men and women of the choir in a lower one: when they sang, the whole congregation turned to face them.

An organ was installed at the end of 1827, and first played in January of the following year by the newly-appointed organist, George Wilkins, who had travelled with it by boat from Bristol to seek the job. The baptismal registers show that, having settled in Ilfracombe, he proceeded to father a large family. During the course of the 19th century the organ was repaired and enlarged several times.

Gratiana Chanter's description of carol singing in her childhood, during the 1860s, is reminiscent of Kenneth Grahame's festive field mice, who call on Mole, in *The Wind in the Willows*.

In old days there was no lack of 'Waits' in Ilfracombe, and long before Christmas they met together to practise the fine old anthems and carols, which had been handed down from father to son for generations. There were the Prices, Germans, Challacombes and Conibears; all had been 'singing families' for generations; and there was old Galliver with his bass viol to lead them. ['Old Galliver' was probably the H. Galliver who in 1826, according to the churchwardens' accounts, was being instructed to play the violincello by Mr. Webber; the latter received three guineas for the task.] 'One party of 'Waits' always sang outside the dining room window on Christmas Eve while the family was at dinner; to them the children carried oranges and other dainties. But the party who came in the middle of the night were by far the most exciting in the children's eyes, for it necessitated being huddled out of beds into shawls and other wraps, and to be sat in the deep window-sills of the rooms overlooking the drive. There, peeping from behind the blinds, they could see the dusky forms below, by the light of their horn lanterns, and how their faces used to glow. Then, after much scuffling, clearing of throats and conversational mumblings, would come the exciting tum, tum, tum, from Gallivers's bass viol. A voice would then say on one note, with great rapidity, 'While Shepherds watched their flocks by night'; then they would start launching forth into marvellous intricacies of song. Here a treble voice would take the solo, clear and strong, then a tenor with many turns and quavers, then the whole body would join in with a real burst of harmony.

Chapter Seven

SALUBRIOUS AIR AND WATERS

FOR CENTURIES the sea dominated Ilfracombe's life by offering its people a livelihood, but after the end of the 18th century the livelihood it offered was of a different sort: the era of the watering-place or seaside resort was beginning. The town and its population were increasing fairly rapidly in the early decades of the 19th century. At the time of the census of 1811 there were 1,934 people living in 444 houses; by 1841 there were 3,679 people living in 795 houses. A small but growing number of householders had discovered a useful source of income: the letting of lodgings.

Ilfracombe had, in fact, begun to be known as a pleasant resort before the end of the 18th century. Although T. H. Cornish wrote, in 1828, that in the 1780s few people had known of any part of north Devon as a beauty spot ('the boldest and, perhaps, the most beautiful variety of picturesque and highly finished scenery old England calls her own') because of the bad old roads, items in the Exeter *Flying Post* suggest otherwise. As early as 1771 the issue for 2 August included an announcement dated 26 July:

> Arrived here, for the Benefit of the Air, Salt Water and to fpend Part of the Summer Seaſon, Mifs McDonald, Mrs. Pynes, Mrs. Knot, Mrs. Hill, Mrs. Spurway and Mrs. Servant; Captain Fraine and Family will be here Tomorrow; Captain Vallarot, who had fpent fome time here, intends to fet off for Gibraltar, where his Regiment now is. Of the very many Perfons who had frequented Ilfracomb for their Health, during the Summer Seafon, for Years paft, but one have died, fo salubrious is its Air and Waters.

By 1788 the *Flying Post* was reporting the town 'remarkably full of genteel company, being resorted to by members of very respectable families from most parts of the country. What pleases strangers most is the conveniency of the bathing machines, and the great attention of the townspeople to accommodate them'.

Three years later the *Universal British Directory* was describing Ilfracombe as 'a pleasant and convenient place for bathing and much resorted to by gentry for that purpose'. The long years of war with France, when moneyed Englishmen could not travel abroad, stimulated interest in seaside holidays, and Ilfracombe, even if it was not as popular as some of the south Devon resorts, had a fair share of the growing industry. By 1805 an indignant-sounding advertiser was announcing:

44

Whereas many ladies and gentlemen have been disappointed of being accommodated with genteel Lodgings, owing to the misrepresentation of an innkeeper at Ilfracombe, who has been in the practise of recommending fuch Lodgings only as fhe pleafes, by which means feveral families have this Summer been difsappointed; the vifitors of this delightful watering place are therefore moft refpectfully informed, that families, with their fervants, may be accommodated (if but for one night only, or any length of time they think proper) to their entire fatisfaction, at No. 1, 2 and 3, Lee's New Buildings, in the centre of the town, at a fhort diftance from the bathing place. Good coachhouses, excellent stabling, etc., adjoining above buildings.

From two water colours he painted in 1811—or at least based on sketches made in that year—we know that the great landscape painter Turner visited Ilfracombe. As the popularity of the English seaside holiday grew, printers began to bring out topographical prints of many coastal places that visitors might buy as souvenirs, or collections over which they might browse at home. Turner accepted a commission to produce a series of water colours in order that an engraver named W. B. Cooke might base engravings on them; they were published in book form as *Picturesque Views on the Southern Coast of England*. Turner was in his thirties, and already an R.A., when he undertook this task. In preparation for it he travelled some 600 miles and made more than 200 pencil sketches.

11. The Capstone, much as it would have looked when Fanny Burney had her 'Adventure terrific on the Rock at Ilfracomb!!!!' 26 years before the Parade was cut.

His father was a Devon man, and Turner himself claimed to have been born in Barnstaple, although as his baptism was registered in London, his biographers discount this. However, on his 1811 visit to what he liked to call his native county, he called on one of his uncles who, like his South Molton grandfather, was a saddler; on his way from Clovelly to Ilfracombe he spent a day at the *Castle* inn, Barnstaple, and visited another uncle who was Master of the Poor house in the town.

At Ilfracombe he made sketches from which he later painted 'Ilfracombe: storm and shipwreck', a marvellously wild impression of a ship driven in on the rocks among fountaining breakers, and 'Ilfracombe from Hillsborough'. It would be in keeping with his character if he put up at the *Packet* inn on the quay, and spent an evening listening to the talk of seamen.

Fairly early in the 19th century, arrivals included some who were not, strictly speaking, on holiday: groups of Oxford or Cambridge undergraduates spending the Long Vacations with a tutor as members of reading parties. In 1817 one such group included a young man of 23 who had been reading mathematics at Cambridge for three years, and was due to take his finals the following January. He was Alexander d'Arblay; he arrived on 1 July from Bath, with his mother, who did her best during the three months they spent in the town not to let it be known that she was celebrated as the author Fanny Burney, whose novels *Evelina*, *Camilla* and *Cecilia* had been avidly read, in the late 18th century, by thousands in all ranks of British society, from royalty downwards.

12.   The *Royal Clarence Hotel* as it appeared c.1890. It was formerly known as *Sutton's Hotel*. Fanny Burney stayed in one of the adjoining houses in 1817. From a guide book, *Ilfracombe: a Resort for all Seasons of the Year*.

She came, she said, as a 'flapper'. Her use of the word was unlike that of the 1920s; she meant that she had to act as a spur to her son, encouraging and supporting him in his studies. It was essential that he should 'assiduously and vigorously pursue a strait line to his Degree', yet she complained that she was occupied from morning to night in stopping the meanderings of his 'Zig Zag Fancies'. (In the event she need not have worried: evidently possessing an innate talent for mathematics, he was to graduate tenth Wrangler, and shortly afterwards became a Fellow of Christ's College.)

Fanny Burney was devoted to her husband, General d'Arblay, the French émigré she had married when she was forty-one. He was in France at this time, partly for his health (he was, in fact, mortally ill) and partly on business. She wrote to him almost daily, and in her letters to him and to relations and friends in England, gives a lively set of impressions of a visitor's summer season in the Ilfracombe of 1817.

Even her account of her journey from Bath to Ilfracombe has its interest as a reminder of the tedium of travel in the early 19th century. She and Alexander set out by 'Diligence' (stage coach), having heard 'such disagreeable histories of the badness of the road', between nine and ten on the morning of 30 June, breakfasted at Bristol, dined at Bridgwater, and reached Taunton in time for tea. They then travelled all night with one stop at Tiverton, and another, very early in the morning, at South Molton for coffee. Twenty-four hours after starting their journey, they arrived at Barnstaple and had breakfast. For the final stage they took a chaise, which put them down at the *Britannia,* the hotel that still stands on the west side of Ilfracombe harbour, where they dined.

That afternoon they found themselves lodgings on the quay at the house of a Mrs. Blackmore, 'widow of some Master of a vessel that traded at Ilfracombe, with Ireland, chiefly', who kept a grocer's shop. They had 'a pretty little Drawing Room, and 2 Bedrooms on the first floor'. Fanny enjoyed the outlook: 'the marine operations proved very amusing, from the coming in and going out of vessels, the lading and unlading, the Ebb and flow of the tide, and the appearing one hour to be so near the sea as to seem but in a Cabin, preparing for sailing with some squadron, and the next beholding the surrounding vessels themselves all on dry land . . . one minute children are playing, Dogs barking and Horses or Asses dragging luggage on a spot where, the next, they could not remain a second without being immersed in salt water'.

She was especially fascinated by what she described as a Spanish ship; in fact, it was a Portuguese schooner, bound for Havanna, detained because an English member of her crew had claimed, mistakenly, that brandy had been smuggled ashore from her. The captain was on parole, but stayed aboard, not trusting his ship out of his sight. He had dismissed his crew, except for the doctor—who doubled as his interpreter—his own servant, his cook and two ship's boys, one of them an American. The cook's activities fascinated Fanny: every morning at about seven be began to prepare a vast *pot au feu* on deck, putting in carrots, onions, turnips, herbs, chicory, garlic (the chicory and garlic, one may suspect, were added from Fanny's imagination), ham and one-pound portions of other meat. Separately, he made 'a Porridge of Potatoes well mashed, and Barley well boiled, with some other ingredient that, when it is poured into a Pan, bubbles up like a syllabub'. When he had finished he made the two boys swab the deck from end to end.

On the night of 6 July there was a tremendous summer storm, and Fanny and Alexander were called to watch two ships in distress. One was trying to make its way into the harbour and the other was standing off, apparently towards Wales. People ran up Lantern Hill with lights (as it was summer, the lantern was not lit) and a boat went out to try to help, but was driven back by the rough seas. Fanny became very alarmed when she saw Alexander high up on the hill, supposing him about to be blown into the sea by what she termed the hurricane. She heard later that one ship made its way safely to Ireland, but the other was lost.

Two days later, helped by Alexander's serious-minded young tutor, Edmund Jacob, she went in search of other lodgings; Jacob had advised a change, warning her that in the harbour area there were at times 'exhalations not healthy'. She moved to a house in the High Street owned by a shoemaker named Ramsay, who possessed several other properties in the town. He had three daughters who helped in the house; the two older girls were 'well-behaved, well-dressed and pleasing', and the youngest was cheerful and talkative, repeatedly making excuses to go into Fanny's apartments to gossip. Her naivety amused the guest; one day she produced a piece of paper she had found on the stairs, saying, 'It must be your young Gentleman's for I can't make out a word of it; for, not thinking of its being Greek, I was going to see what it was about; but all the letters are writ the wrong way, so I suppose the young Gentleman's to put them right'. The paper bore calculations in algebra!

From her drawing-room window Fanny could see the Capstone, crowned then with a weather vane on a tall pole in the form of a salmon, 'enormously large, painted to the life upon Iron'. Her descriptions of Ilfracombe in her letters are not flattering. To her husband she wrote 'Town it is called, because it has a market; else, many villages might dispute its title to that honour. It consists only of what might be called, in Geographic Language, a *Neck of Street,* for it is one long run of houses, opposite to each other, that descend from a high Hill, Zig Zag, now narrow, now broader (never *broad*) that leads from the Church to Quay without uniformity, prettiness, or neatness. It has no sort of public building, nor any trade or commerce'. Nevertheless it had its coasting trade, as she admits by going on: 'It exists by its sea-intercourse with Ireland and Wales, to both which countries passage vessels pass continually. But though *The Street* is so unadorned, the backs of almost all the Houses are open, on one side, to country prospects, and on the other to the Sea. We have entirely avoided the Street in our apartments, which look upon high Hills, and an angle of the Ocean, by which we can behold all the Vessels that pass to and from Bristol and Ireland, or Wales'.

Not only were the houses 'built of stone hewn out of the neighbouring Rocks, uncouth and rude', but 'many parts of the Town and its vicinity are mere Rocks. This occasions but little Wood, and robs the views, therefore, in general, of that

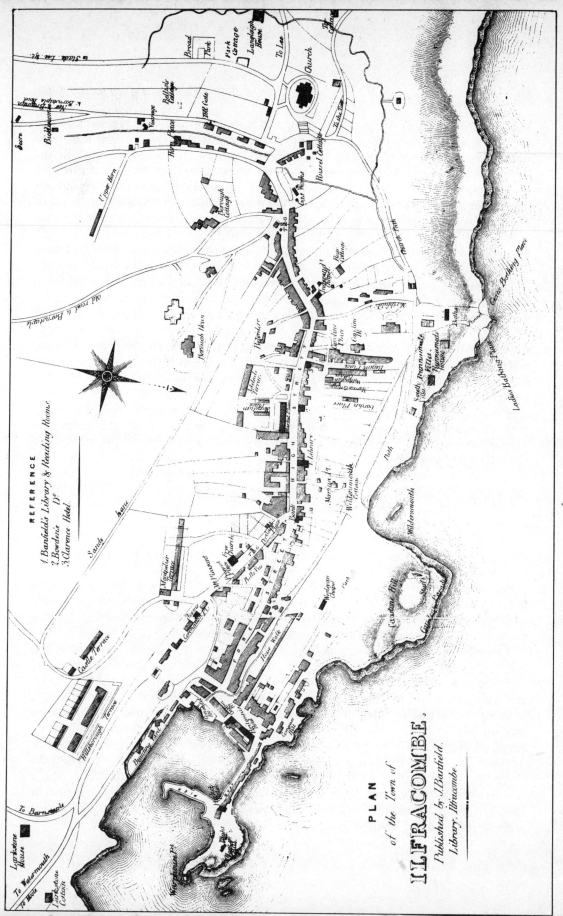

PLAN
of the Town of
ILFRACOMBE.

Published by J.Banfield.
Library. Ilfracombe.

REFERENCE
1. Banfield's Library & Reading Rooms.
2. Bowden's Do.
3. Clarence Hotel.

13. A town plan of Ilfracombe included in *A Guide to Ilfracombe and the Neighbouring Towns* published by J. Banfield in the 1830s.

luxurious branch of village decoration'. Moreover, although there were pretty villages not far away, the roads to them were poor. 'Four years ago, there was not a Chaise to be had in this town, but the report of the rural charms of the situation having, of late, brought many visitors, some for retirement, others for oeconomy [sic], there is now a hotel established, whence all common necessities for travelling may now be procured'. (This was *Sutton's* hotel, next door to the house where Fanny was staying.)

She did not find Ilfracombe as cheap as she had heard it was; only a few years ago 'all provisions, Lodgings, and coals, were then so cheap, that a whole and large family might live here for less than the simplest single man can live at Paris—in London—or at Bath. But the secret of cheapness was no sooner whispered from Friend to Friend, than it was buzzed in society, and heard by the common swarm, who now Hive themselves here for oeconomy. But the Multitude has warped what the Individual had enjoyed, and nothing now is marvellous in cheapness, though nothing has attained the excellence appertaining to dearness: for the Market is ill supplied, the poultry is lean and ill-fed, not a single Lodging house has a pump or a cistern, and currants and gooseberries are the only Fruits cultivated'. (Elsewhere she contradicts this by describing the garden of her landlord where flowers, vegetables and fruits mingled in profusion, and where not only currants and gooseberries but strawberries, raspberries, apples, pears and plums were grown.) 'Even those, this year, have never ripened. All of other sorts come from Barnstaple, eleven miles off. The meat has by no means the *fine* flavour of the pasture near Bath, and there is Fish very precariously, and of no variety'.

After the sheltered air of Bath, she found Ilfracombe 'a very mere summer residence: it is North, and covered with sea breezes, which whistle around me from Morn to Night, and roar out aloud from Night to Morn'. And what was perhaps worse, the town was not only 'behind hand for Convenience or elegance' but 'Science, Literature and the arts are all out of the question'.

However, she kept busy, struggling to overcome what she called Alexander's 'disgust to his enforced study' and also sorting and arranging the correspondence of her father, the eminent musician, Dr. Charles Burney, in preparation for the memoir of him she was to publish in 1832.

Towards the end of her stay in Ilfracombe she went out one morning, knowing her son to be at work with his tutor, and walked down to Wildersmouth. The tide was low; it must have been about on the turn, but she supposed it to be still going out, and wandered across the rocks around the foot of the Capstone, looking for attractive pebbles for General d'Arblay, who had developed an interest in mineralogy. Somehow she got cut off by the tide, and climbed out of reach of the waves. At that time Capstone Parade had not been cut, and evidently no one was within hearing or sight; she was marooned until dusk, according to the long and minutely detailed and dramatic account of her experience which she wrote six years later for a friend's amusement. At the time she noted in her journal for 24 September 1817, 'Adventure terrific on a Rock at Ilfracomb!' and the following day added 'Abandonne [sic] on the Rock at Ilfracomb!!!!!'

Eventually her son and one of his undergraduate friends sighted her and she was guided to safety by an old sailor with a lantern. It is clear that she was never in nearly as much danger as her probably fictionally-heightened account suggests. And it is useless to go in search of the exact place where she climbed up: she visited it two days later, and already, she says, 'A. Storm of equinoctial violence had broken off its pyramidal height, and the Draft of Sand and Gravel and fragments of Rock had given a new face to the whole Recess'.

Her stint as a flapper at an end, she was back in her beloved Bath by 5 October. General d'Arblay, returned from France, joined her in a few days, and she nursed him devotedly for the last six months of his life. Later she was to write that 1817 had been the last happy year of her life.

Chapter Eight

'THE BRIGHTON OF NORTH DEVON'

TEN YEARS after Fanny Burney's visit, the Duchess of Clarence, wife of the future William IV, arrived in Ilfracombe on a Sunday evening. Prince William Henry, Duke of Clarence, the sailor prince who was by this time Lord High Admiral, had sailed from Plymouth to inspect the fleet at Milford Haven, but the Duchess disliked sea voyages, and preferred the shortest possible crossing. Leaving Plymouth, she had travelled to Heanton Satchville, where she had been the guest of Lord Clinton. At Barnstaple she had changed horses at the *Golden Lion,* and acknowledged 'the astounding acclamations that rent the air' from the huge crowd filling the streets. She was expected to reach Ilfracombe by six in the evening; early in the afternoon 'the town began to assume a very gay and lively appearance', and here, too, most of the inhabitants turned out. Fifty special constables had been appointed to regulate them.

The street was decorated with triumphal arches covered in flowers, evergreens, flags and crowns, and 20 sailors in blue jackets and white trousers waited to take the horses from the Duchess's carriage and, with the North Devon band marching in front, pull it to Mill House, the home of James (later Sir James) Meek, a public servant who owned a considerable acreage of agricultural land around Ilfracombe, as well as its mill—roughly at the foot of today's Mill Head—the surrounding meadows and gardens and part of Ropery Meadow.[1]

The following morning, after a very early breakfast, Meek escorted the Duchess, again with the band in attendance, along the Rope Walk and through a private garden to the pier, where two steamships, the *Meteor* and the *Comet,* were waiting. 'The inhabitants of the lower, were not less loyal and attentive to Her Royal Highness than those of the upper part of the town, as everyone testified their loyal attachment by spreading carpets, strewing flowers, erecting triumphal arches and flying numerous flags', reported the *North Devon Journal.*

The Duchess, having expressed her satisfaction at the manner in which she had been received, and left 20 guineas to be divided among those 'in subordinate offices' who had looked after her, boarded the *Meteor* at about 7.30 a.m., her departure saluted by the guns of the harbour and those of the revenue cutter in the offing.

To prevent themselves from feeling flat after these excitements, the towns-people held a public dinner in the Rope Walk, where 'some hundreds of persons were regaled with good old English fare', and the day ended with a ball at the public rooms in Coronation Terrace 'and other enjoyments and amusements highly gratifying to everyone present'.

Coronation Terrace, high on the hillside above the harbour, had not long been built (the most recent coronation having been that of George IV in 1820) and the Rooms, as they were usually called, with their 'neat Ionic facade', ballroom, billiards and reading rooms, gave the town great satisfaction; they provided the sort of fashionable meeting place that had been lacking. A number of other elegant terraces were built in the first decade of the 19th century, several of them with names that link them closely to their time: Regent and Coburg Terraces, Waterloo and Wellington Terraces, and in due course Adelaide Terrace, in honour of the Duchess who became queen in 1830.

According to Thomas Cornish, whose *Sketch of the Rise and Progress of the Principal Towns of the North of Devon* was published in 1828,[2] (with a fulsome dedication to Sir Bourchier Wrey) various 'families of distinction' lingered late in the 1827 season, possibly because a rumour had gone round that the Duke of Wellington, then Prime Minister, was soon to arrive on a visit. However, this proved to be no more than a rumour.

Cornish wrote with enthusiasm of the 'capacious and handsome' houses of Coronation Terrace, and the magnificence of the view from there and from Montpelier Terrace, a little higher to the west; the prospect of the Bristol Channel coast was not only 'all that we deem romantic, grand and lovely'; it was full of activity, showing 'the types of industry, the invention and the commercial importance of Britain—fishing boats, vessels of every size and description from the Pill pilot boat up to the West India merchantman and the line of battle ship. Steamers and pleasure yachts crowd the coast in every direction during the summer months, in quick succession. The constant and rapid communication with Ireland, Wales and Bristol, has wrought a surprising change . . . of late, and since the different steam packets have been plying from Bristol, Swansea and so on, the busy bustling scenes of arrivals and departures have been witnessed with no small gratification by the authorities'. All in all, Cornish declared, 'the increasing celebrity of this romantic and marine spot is, we are well informed, without a precedent . . . it is the Brighton of Barnstaple and the North of Devon'.

There had been sea bathing at Wildersmouth and the outer harbour from the late 18th century, and bathing machines were provided. Fanny Burney had remarked that at Wildersmouth there was only room for one machine, but this was not always the case. A tourists' guide of 1819[3] stated that 'Many bathing machines stand outside the pier', which presumably means that they were towed there at low tide, since at high tide they would have been under water outside or inside the pier.

Some people thought that there should be provision for indoor bathing. Among them was Thomas Stabb, a surgeon who had moved to Ilfracombe from Torquay in 1823. With John Banfield, a bookseller who was a son-in-law of the inventor Richard Trevithick, Stabb gathered support for the formation of the Ilfracombe Sea Bathing Company, which built the attractive little Greek Revival baths which still stand at the entrance to the Tunnels beaches. At about the same time the Tunnels themselves were cut into and under the then open green hillside of the Runnacleave to reach the two small beaches of fine silvery shillet, one on either side of a rocky projection that allowed for a discreet segregation of sexes: as a writer of 1840 put it, 'the westward part is allotted to Gentlemen, while the Eastward is by custom left to the Ladies and is carefully guarded against all intrusion. Machines and bathing women are in attendance, and every information respecting the proper time to bathe will be given at the Baths'. (Segregation lasted a long time; not until 1905 was mixed bathing allowed at the Tunnels.)

Banfield remarked, in the first edition of the guide book to Ilfracombe which he published in the late 1830s, that 'the ground around the Baths is well calculated for dwelling houses'. The map included in the second edition of his book, however, shows that only Runnamede House and Runnamede Villa (presumably the level meadow below the Runnacleave was once the Runna Meadow) had at that time been built within a 100-yard radius of the Baths.

The roughly contemporary tithe map shows that the greater part of Ilfracombe and its surrounding farms was owned by not more than 20 people, four of them women. During the years between 1811 and 1851, over 400 houses were built in Ilfracombe, many of them in the terraces already mentioned. The population, having almost exactly doubled since the beginning of the century, stabilised briefly between 1841 and 1851, partly because of some emigration from the area, before beginning another rapid rise. The High Street, of which Fanny Burney had been so critical, had been widened during the late 1830s; a number of handsome houses had been built, with fashionable shop fronts.

14. The Baths, built in 1836 by the Ilfracombe Sea Bathing Co. The opening of the Tunnels may be seen on the right, and the West Wilder Brook—now wholly hidden away underground except in some private gardens—flows beneath the bridge in the foreground.

It was possible by this time for all new houses in the town to be built with fittings for gas lighting; after organising indoor bathing facilities, Stabb and Banfield at once proceeded to form the Ilfracombe Gas Company, which built gas works at the back of Church Street in 1837.

From 1813, fathers' occupations were entered in the baptismal registers. In the next 24 years, up to the accession of Queen Victoria, there were 1,859 baptisms; almost exactly one-third of these were of children whose fathers described themselves as master mariners or mariners. Yet by 1850 only 26 master mariners are recorded in White's *Directory*. Nevertheless, the registers show that many men's occupations were still concerned with the sea: shipbuilder (and also boatbuilder, shipwright and shipsmith), chandler, ropemaker, anchorsmith, and sailmaker all appear. Remarkably, only one man calls himself a fisherman; perhaps some of the captains and owners of fishing boats preferred to set themselves down as master mariners. There were several coastguards and revenue men, and the name of the local coastguard cutter, H.M.S. *Harpy,* appears a number of times, as children were born to members of her crew.

Officers of the Royal Navy, the army and the East India Company—retired. presumably—were living in the town, as well as an increasing number of those who gave no occupation, entering themselves as 'Gentlemen'. The three groups with most representatives, after those with marine associations, were labourers, yeomen and farmers, and carpenters, but some 60 trades appeared, including a huntsman, a gamekeeper, a bee-keeper, a tinker, and someone who combined the trades of umbrella-maker and bell-hanger.

In view of the amount of building going on, it is slightly surprising that there were only four builders in the town in 1850, according to White, though he lists also 12 stonemasons and plasterers, six carpenters, three painters and glaziers, and two timber and slate merchants.

There were still only three hotels: the former *Sutton's,* now the *Royal Clarence,* and two founded in the 18th century, the *Packet*, by the pier, and the *Britannia.* But there were 15 public houses, nine of them in the High Street—the *London, Exeter* and *Barnstaple* inns, the *Moon,* the *Star* and the *Rising Sun,* the *Lamb,* the *Wellington* and the *Ring of Bells.* The number of lodging houses, on the other hand, was increasing with each decade: in 1830 the names of only 18 were included in Pigot and Co.'s *National Commercial Directory*; by 1866 the *Post Office Directory* was listing more than 130, many of them in the new terraces or the High Street.

The 1819 tourists' guide observed that 'Packets are constantly passing to Bristol, Swansea and Milford; and good skiffs may be procured in an instant'. Would-be voyagers, it appears, might hail a packet as later travellers would hail a bus, being rowed out swiftly from the harbour and taken aboard a short distance offshore. Some twenty years later, Banfield said that the Cornish steamers called *off* the harbour on their way to and from Bristol.

However, in 1822 a steam packet sailing from Bristol to Cork, the *Duke of Lancaster,* began to call *at* Ilfracombe, and this was the start of the port's regular sea link for passengers wishing to reach Bristol or parts of South Wales in a fraction of the time taken by the stage coaches. In addition to giving information about the Cornish steamers, Banfield was able to inform his readers that 'Steam Packets ply between Ilfracombe and Bristol throughout the year, and Ilfracombe and Swansea, from May to October'.

Communications by road had, however, improved somewhat by the 1830s. New highways had been cut from Exeter and Taunton to Barnstaple, and continued to Ilfracombe soon afterwards. Whereas in 1819 there had been a coach to Barnstaple only three times a week, there was now a daily service of coaches and horse-drawn omnibuses. For travellers who wanted to make their own arrangements, 'Post Chaises, Cars and Saddle Horses are easily procured at the Inns or Livery Stables', Banfield assured his readers, while for less demanding journeys, 'Sedans, Bath Chairs, Ponies and Donkeys are to be hired in many parts of the town'.

15. The Capstone, showing the Parade, cut in 1843, from Gadsby.

By 1843 the *North Devon Journal* was able to report complacently in midsummer that, 'we are happy to announce that visitors are pouring into this fashionable watering place . . . We have never enjoyed greater facilities of communication than at present. We have coaches to and from Barnstaple four times a day, which bring us passengers from London, Northern, Bristol, Exeter and Plymouth coaches, and we have frequent steamers from Wales, Bristol and Hayle which ply at exceedingly moderate fares'.

That autumn a new attraction for holidaymakers, a walk around the Capstone (which had been cut largely to give work to a number of unemployed men) was opened with a public tea 'in a commodious tent erected on the parade', fireworks, and two balls at the Rooms, one of them for tradesmen. The workers had toiled throughout the previous winter to move huge quantities of rock, at a total cost of £220, raised by private subscriptions of the gentry and residents. A correspondent in a local paper approved the gentle slope of the Walk, 'so suitable for bathchairs'.

Some idea of what a visitor had to pay for lodgings, food and general expenses, once arrived, may be gathered from a diary kept by a businessman, Daniel Benham, who spent at least two·summer holidays in the town.[4] In 1849 he, his wife and daughter, Anne, visited South Devon, Weston-super-Mare and Bristol before embarking on the small steamer *Torridge* for Ilfracombe. (The *Torridge* was advertised as the only steamer that landed and embarked passengers without the need to use boats; in those days, before the building of the long promenade pier in the early 1870s, larger vessels had to lie off the harbour entrance.) They left Bristol at about 11 a.m. and did not reach Ilfracombe until 8 p.m., after a queasy crossing with 'a ground swell at right angles with the wind'.

They found temporary lodgings with a Mrs. Cockburn, near the *Britannia* hotel, and Benham noted down his day's expenses: steamboat 39 shillings, fly two shillings and sixpence, porters two shillings, stewards two shillings and sixpence, Mrs. Cockburn three shillings. After two days they rented apartments on the Quay for 30 shillings a week for the three of them (Mrs. Cockburn's charge was nine shillings for the two nights, with a penny-halfpenny for baths.)

Although Benham records what he paid for a wide variety of items, from meat, fowls and wine to bacon, rice and biscuits, he does not usually give the quantities bought, so in this respect his diary is not a very useful guide to prices. However, a contemporary market report in the *North Devon Journal* shows that beef and mutton were fivepence halfpenny to sixpence a pound, butter ninepence, chickens two shillings to two shillings and fourpence a couple, ducks two shillings and two shillings and eightpence. Eggs were 16 for a shilling, potatoes sixpence to sevenpence a peck, and flatfish sixpence to eightpence a pound. Fruit and vegetables were said to be plentiful and cheap: beans, for instance, were one penny a pound. Laundry, at two shillings and a penny a week, was a comparatively expensive item, but no doubt this included the washing of a large quantity of linen and clothes.

Benham had his hair cut for sixpence by the only hairdresser in the town, or so he says, although White lists two. One of his reasons for visiting Ilfracombe was to seek improved health: he speaks of being oppressed by the weak state of his nerves, of feeling very poorly and weak, and sometimes mentions a headache or an upset stomach. On one occasion he consulted a Mr. Tuckett, who prescribed for him; the medicine cost two shillings and eightpence. At other times he bought unspecified pills.

The Benhams were devout Nonconformists, and frequently attended the Independent or the Wesleyan chapel; once Benham put ten shillings in the collection in aid of the London Missionary Society.

On a visit to Barnstaple by the 'Faithful' van they were delayed by an accident of the sort that was not uncommon in the days when vehicles were often drawn by overworked and underfed horses: 'the poor animal fell and broke one of the shafts of the van and cut both its own shins'. Having reached Barnstaple by 12.30, the Benhams had a meal at Weedon's Eating House in Bedford Street; for a shilling each they ate boiled round of beef, mutton chops, beans and rice, and drank Indian pale ale.

During their stay in Ilfracombe they made expeditions to all the places holidaymakers usually visited. One that was perhaps slightly out of the ordinary was to Combe Martin, 'where we had explained to us the process of melting ore, most of which is brought from Cornwall'. Having tipped the smelters a shilling, Benham brought away 'two small specimens of the Cornish ore which yields 15½ hundredweights of metal to each ton of ore'.[5]

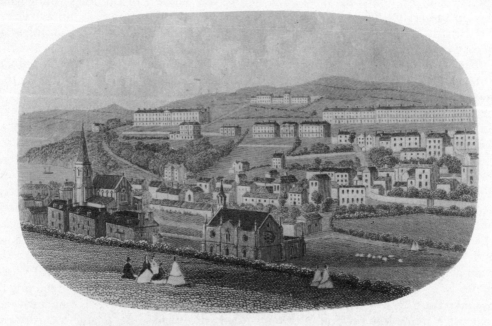

16.   Ilfracombe in 1865, from Gadsby, showing the terraces built in the previous 35 years, which George Eliot saw as 'factory-like lines of buildings'.

By 1852, when the Benhams again arrived in Ilfracombe, the British Steam Navigation Company was advertising a reduction of fares on its powerful paddle steamers, *Star* and *Phoenix*. Boat cabins cost eight shillings (servants, six shillings), while a fore cabin was only four shillings. One advantage of these ships was that those who wanted to transport their vehicles and horses could do so—at a price: one pound for a gig, two for a carriage, and one pound for each horse.

This time the family took a train from Paddington on 27 July at 10.15 a.m., and arrived at Swansea at 7 p.m. Finding it 'a smoky hole', they decided to catch the *Princess Royal* steamer at four the next morning. She was screw-propelled, not a paddler, and made the crossing in three and a half hours, on a calm sea, though several people managed to be seasick, including Ann Benham. Having been rowed ashore, the Benhams had breakfast at the *Steam Packet* hotel and found lodgings at No. 3 Sea View Cottages, where they paid twenty-four shillings for two bedrooms and a sitting-room.

A few days after their arrival an excursion party from Wales landed from a steamer. 'They seemed as wild as their mountains and as haggard-looking as their smelting furnaces could make them', Benham observed. However, 'in their behaviour there was as much decorum as could be expected'.

On this visit Benham mentions the market, which was on a Saturday, as it still is; he noted that it was 'pretty well as usual supplied with fruit and vegetables from the surrounding countryside. Meat from Barnstaple, i.e. beef and veal, the shopkeepers of the town having stalls for the sale of shoes, crockery, glass, bacon, cheese, etc.'. A local joke he records was that the market began at 12 and left off at noon.

17. Hillsborough Terrace, from Gadsby. Beatrix Potter stayed in one of these houses, when on holiday with her parents as a girl of fifteen.

One of his holiday occupations was copying out inscriptions in the churchyard. His wife and daughter, on the other hand, enjoyed weeding the garden of their lodgings, from which, when they had had enough of weeding, they could go down to the beach and climb over the rocks to Lantern Hill. All three frequently attended morning and evening chapel services. They walked to such places as Hillsborough, Slade and the Cairn (still evidently known as the Carn), but for longer expeditions hired some kind of horse-drawn vehicle: a four-wheeled chaise to drive to Watermouth and Berrynarbor along 'the new road lately made by

Mr. Basset, the lord of the manor'; a *britsky* (an open carriage with a hooded top, the name coming from the Polish 'britzka') to visit Braunton and Lee. They do not seem to have tried that very popular form of transport in 19th-century Ilfracombe, the donkey, though Benham does mention a walk to Lee Lane on which he first met a boy on a donkey with a mail bag on his back and then was overtaken by three parties on donkeys, one of which was composed of 'a male and three female Friends (Quakers) whose costume gave a rather grotesque appearance to the scene'. (In 1816 a visitor to Ilfracombe, the Revd. Woolocombe, observed that 'all wheel conveyance at that time was done by donkey chairs, and very proud and dignified their occupants looked as, turning their heads first to one side and then to the other, they proceeded slowly along the streets and lanes of the place, with a deliberate look at all they passed'.

Benham used his diary as a sort of scrapbook, sticking in engravings of Ilfracombe and Barnstaple, church and chapel notices of one sort and another, and concert programmes. Concerts, held at the Public Rooms in Coronation Terrace, began at eight in the evening and finished at ten. One featured 'the Infant Alice, five years old, and Miss May, in a Gondola Duet', but does not say whether the Infant Alice sang or played an instrument. There were other soirees at the Rooms, beginning at eight; dancing continued until midnight. Banfield sold subscription tickets for the set of six soirees held during the season, at a guinea' each; non-subscribers paid 2s. 6d. a time. The committee which organised these events was headed by Sir Bourchier Palk Wrey, the lord of the manor, and the surgeon, Thomas Stabb, was a member, as he was of so many things.

Towards the end of the Benham's 1849 holiday, there had been an outbreak of cholera in the town. This particular epidemic had begun in 1848 and spread throughout Britain. On their return in 1852 the Benhams were told by the sexton that about 80 people had been carried off in three weeks. This suggests the sort of graveyard gloom proper to his calling, but the burial registers for the parish church show that he was not exaggerating unduly. The number of burials in Holy Trinity during the years 1847–1851, excluding 1849, averaged about 55 a year.[6] In 1849, until the end of July, there were 33 deaths, including six octogenarians and six infants aged from a few months to two years.

In August nine died, among them two infants and another octogenarian, and in September there were 34 deaths. (At some later date, presumably, the vicar, the Revd. Chanter, wrote at the foot of one page: 'Note: This was the year when Ilfracombe was visited by Cholera'.) During the next three months there were 48 burials, when ordinarily there might have been only a dozen or so.

In his diary Benham stoutly called the illness croup, and, encouraged by his wife, refused to be alarmed into cutting short his holiday. However, he did preserve a leaflet headed 'The Cholera', which gave a form of prayer to be used 'in all churches and chapels throughout those parts of the United Kingdom called England and Ireland, instead of the prayer used during any time of common plague and sickness, on Sunday, the 16th of September: to be continued during the prevalence of the cholera in this country; for obtaining pardon for our sins and, particularly, for beseeching God to remove from us

18. Looking out across Wildersmouth beach to the Torrs in about 1840, 'when meadows stretched from the church to the Quay, and the scythes clinked merrily in the early mornings when the hay harvest came'. Lundy may be seen in the distance. (By G. Rowe.)

that grievous disease with which many places in the kingdom are visited'. The prayer went on to beg that petitioners might be preserved from, among other things, 'intestine commotions'.

A visitor to Ilfracombe in that year of 1849 who took cholera seriously and urged local authorities to tighten up their 'sanitary slackness' was Charles Kingsley. He came to the town at the beginning of the year in a state of complete nervous exhaustion. According to his latest biographer, Susan Chitty,[7] he had been doing virtually four jobs at once: running his parish of Eversley in Hampshire single-handed because he could not afford a curate, helping to launch a weekly publication, *Politics for the People,* lecturing on English Literature at Queen's College, and writing his novel *Yeast,* the first instalment of which appeared anonymously in *Fraser's Magazine* in July 1848. As his doctor advised complete change and rest, he moved his family to Ilfracombe, where he had spent a year of his boyhood immediately before his father had been offered the living at Clovelly. The first house they rented was not to the liking of his wife, Fanny, but after a short search she decided that Runnymede Villa was 'a perfect bijou of a place having everything that could be wished for except a view of the sea'.

In April Kingsley wrote to thank his father for providing a locum for him during his absence:

> I now am better than I have been at all, I may say. A tremendous gale of wind has acted on me exactly like champagne and cathedral organs in one, and restored my (what you would call nervous) what I call magnetic tone. I am quite ashamed of amusing myself here while you are toiling for me; but being here, I will not do things by halves, and am leading a truly hoggish life—viz: 18 hours sleeping, 4 hours eating, 2 hours walking, 0 hours reading—24; which you will allow is a change in my dietetics. I went to Morte yesterday, and found, as indeed I do of all this country, that my old childish recollection had painted it, not as usual, larger and more striking than the actuality, but smaller. I find that I was not, as a boy of ten, capable of taking in the grandeur of the scenery here, and that I brought away with me only as much of it as I could hold. Every hill (and this strikes me much) except perhaps little Capstone, is much higher and grander than I thought. I feel the change from Hampshire very much—the world seems upside down. I get a strange swimming in the wits now and then, at seeing farm-houses under my feet, and cows feeding, like so many flies against a wall.

Notwithstanding this, he claimed to find his climbing head surer than ever; he could placidly look over 'the awful gulf of Hillsborough as if it were a six-foot wall'. He was in considerable financial difficulties, caused in part by Fanny's extravagant tastes (she was the daughter of a rich Cornish mine owner, and her family had been against her marrying the gauche, penniless young man who had fallen in love with her literally, he always insisted, at first sight: 'eye-wedlock' he called it.) Writing offered itself as the obvious way to earn money: he set to work on a very long essay (its five sections run to about 25,000 words altogether) for *Fraser's Magazine.* It appeared in July, and it seems that he received only ten pounds for it. In the second section of this essay, 'The Coast Line', he describes himself and a friend, to whom he gives the name of Claude Mellot, a character in *Yeast,* setting off aboard a Clovelly trawling skiff from Lynton at 4 o'clock on a May morning.

It was exceptionally hot for May in Devon. As they drifted down the coast past the Valley of Rocks, Heddon's Mouth and Combe Martin, 'the great sun-roasted fire-brick of the Exmoor range' was burning up the breeze, and Claude was sickening in the heat, despite the calm sea. At last they came to Ilfracombe, 'with its rock-walled harbour, its little wood of masts within, its white terraces rambling up the hills, its Capstone sea-walk, the finest "marine parade", as Cockneydom terms it, in all England, except that splendid Hoe of Plymouth . . . And there is the little isolated rock-chapel, where, 700 years ago, our west-country forefathers used to go to pray to St Nicholas for deliverance from shipwreck—a method lovingly regretted by some, as "a pious idea of the Ages of Faith". We, however, shall prefer the present method of lighthouses and the worthy Trinity Board, as actually more godly and "faithful", as well as more useful and probably so do the sailors themselves'.

He suggested that Claude should go ashore and recover from his queasiness before continuing his tour of north Devon. If you were seasick or heart-sick, or (remembering his own money troubles) pocket-sick, there was no pleasanter or cheaper place of cure, he said, 'than this same Ilfracombe, with its quiet nature and its quiet luxury, its rock fairy-land and its sea-walks, its downs and combes, its kindly people and, if possible, its still kinder climate, which combines the soft warmth of South Devon with the bracing freshness of the Welsh mountains; where winter has slipped out of the list of seasons . . .'.

Chapter Nine

SEASIDE STUDIES

AFTER THE APPALLING OUTBREAK of cholera in the early 1830s which, throughout Britain, caused some 50,000 deaths, parliament moved very slowly towards legislation intended to improve the general standard of public hygiene. It is somewhat ironic that the Public Health Act of 1848 was passed only a short time before the even worse epidemic began in the autumn of that year, the effects of which in Ilfracombe have already been noted. During the next 12 months, more than 53,000 people died in England and Wales alone. In general, Devon suffered comparatively lightly, with 2,366 deaths.[1]

The Act laid down that if more than one-tenth of the rated inhabitants of a town signed a petition, an inspector from the newly-created Board of Health would be sent to conduct an enquiry. In November 1849, such an inspector, Thomas Rammell, arrived in Ilfracombe to hear evidence from a number of leading townspeople concerning the state of the 'sewerage, drainage and supply of water, and the sanitary conditions of the inhabitants of the parish of Ilfracombe'.

Both the ubiquitous Thomas Stabb and a Dr. John Jones, who described himself as the oldest medical man in the town, did their best to persuade the inspector to 'discard from his mind the idea that Ilfracombe was an unhealthy town'. Dr. Jones, observing that he had been in practice there for 32 years, declared that he had never seen a case of primary fever, whatever that was, in his life. When the inspector asked him if he did not consider the recent ravages of cholera were a stigma on a place 'naturally so healthy' he answered no; cholera he regarded as 'a mysterious visitation of Providence'.

Lay members of the public made it clear that they doubted whether Providence was as mysterious as all that: a master mariner named Hooper probably summed up the majority view when he spoke of 'the bad drainage of the town generally; the result of which was that the streets, in summer time especially, were filled with odours more offensive than he had ever smelt in Portugal or Ireland'.

The inspector's report was not published until August 1850. A local newspaper commented that the townspeople had begun to think that the inspector had forgotten them; they 'felt that they must help themselves, and they have been about it'. First they took back into their own hands the care of their streets, previously managed by the Barnstaple Turnpike Trust under an Act of Parliament of 1827, and laid a new drain along the whole length of High Street and Fore Street 'to take out of sight the street surface water and gully-hole exudations'. The wardens of the parish ways raised subscriptions and repaired public walks, and everywhere cleanliness was encouraged, 'so that what with the white-washing, chloridizing, gutter-scrubbing, dung-hill driving, pig-persecuting, cess-pool purging, well-cleansing and sewer-flushing of last winter, and now with this great drainage enterprise nearly finished, sober and considering men stroke their chin (sic) very complacently, satisfied that we are now getting almost decent'.[2]

After all that, the sober and considering men must have been chagrined to read the inspector's report. Even their new main sewer did not obviate one of his chief criticisms, which was that the harbour received the whole of the refuse it carried, as well as that which ran into the Wilder brooks, 'the effluvium sometimes pervading the whole of the lower districts of the town'. He also pointed out that the water supply was insufficient and often of bad quality, since it was drawn from those same Wilder brooks; that there was a deficiency of privy accommodation and that the burial ground was overcrowded; he considered that 'the general character of the health of the district was decidedly low'. Evidently he had not been impressed by the sanguine opinion of Thomas Stabb and Dr. Jones. He recommended that the provisions of the Public Health Act should be applied in the parish and that a local Board of Health should be elected, consisting of nine people drawn from the whole of the district.

A local Board was duly formed in 1851. Thomas Stabb promptly became its first chairman, a position he was to hold for eight years; Dr. John Jones, also a member, was to succeed him in that office. One of the Board's earliest actions was to commission the building of a new sewage works, which was completed in 1853. It also arranged for an improved water supply, drawing from the West Wilder Brook at Slade into a large brick-built tank. Within 15 years this, too, proved inadequate for the growing population, and the first Slade reservoir was constructed to hold nearly 21 million gallons.

The inspector's report had made a distinction between the upper, residential area of the town and the lower, poorer district around the harbour, where dozens of small houses—many simply 'one up and one down'—crowded together. It was still the main working part of the town, with shipbuilding a continuing industry. The shipyard on the south side of the harbour, under a succession of owners, launched 50 small ships in the years from 1800 to 1850. In 1828 William Huxtable had celebrated the visit of the Duchess of Clarence, the previous year, by naming one of his newly-completed ships after her. This wooden vessel of 174 tons was to be no local coaster; bought by Liverpool merchants, she traded as far as the East Indies. The 1850s saw the period of greatest production: under the ownership of Charles Dennis, two ships of over 300 tons were built: the *Kossuth* (renamed the *Maggie*) and the *Coronella*. Both were to make many voyages across the oceans of the world, the first sailing between London and China, and the second to ports in South America.[3]

Once the railway from Exeter reached Barnstaple in 1854, the north coast began to attract a number of visitors who would previously have travelled on to resorts such as Sidmouth and Teignmouth; they had the slight inconvenience of changing to a coach for the last 11 miles, but coach travel was still familiar enough to be no deterrent to most travellers. By July 1856 the *North Devon*

Journal was noting with approval, 'Perhaps this town never presented a more animated aspect than on Monday. There were, it is estimated, full 1,500 visitors occupying lodgings from eight guineas a week to five shillings a week'. (A guide book of about the same time informed its readers that 'First class furnished houses can be obtained here from £100 to £150 per annum; second class, from £60 to £100; third class from £35 to £60. First class lodgings are from £4 to £8 a week; second class from £2 to £4; third class from £1 to £2 . . . a commoner sort can be obtained from 5 shillings a week and upwards'.)[4]

19.   Ilfracombe harbour by G. Townsend, published by H. Besley in 1854. An early paddle steamer lies alongside the pier originally built by the Bourchiers—probably before the mid-15th century—and rebuilt or repaired more than once by their descendants, the Bourchier Wreys.

By this time the era of the seaborne day-dripper had arrived; on that July day in 1856 no fewer than five steamers lay in the outer harbour: they included three wooden paddlers, the *Dart,* which had brought a party from Bute Dock, Cardiff; and the *Lord Beresford* and the *Beaufort,* which had carried a large number from Swansea. Some 500 of these excursionists 'dispread themselves over the locality, and enjoyed themselves, every one after his own taste and humour, but all were well conducted'. They re-embarked for Wales at 4.30 p.m.

In the same issue of the newspaper the Bristol Steam Navigation Company advertised the regular sailings of their iron paddle-steamer, *Prince of Wales,* from Swansea to Ilfracombe on Mondays and Wednesdays, the *Juno* from Bristol on Saturdays and Tuesdays, and the *Princess Royal* steam packet which left Cumberland Basin, Bristol for Lynmouth, Ilfracombe, Appledore, Instow, and Bideford on Tuesdays and Fridays. The fare on the *Princess Royal* was 5s. for deck passengers, 8s. for the saloon.

Later in 1856 Ilfracombe received a visit from a member of the royal family that lasted hardly longer than that of the Duchess of Clarence. The Prince of Wales, the future Edward VII, was then not quite 15, 'not remarkably tall, rather delicately made, and of prepossessing appearance', the *North Devon Journal* reported. With his tutor, a former barrister named Frederick Gibbs, and another attendant, he arrived at Barnstaple by train on an October evening, supposedly incognito, and travelled to Lynton in a fly to spend two nights at the *Castle* hotel.

20. G. Townsend's view of the town from Lantern Hill in 1856. Beyond the Capstone rise the still open slopes of the Runnacleave and the Torrs. High on the left appears Coronation Terrace with the Assembly Rooms in the centre.

The prince and his companions then hired 'three rough ponies' and rode to Ilfracombe on an evening of rain and wind; they arrived at the *Britannia* at 8 p.m. and put up there. After a walk on the top of the Capstone the next morning, where he appeared 'much pleased with the extensive views and grand scenery'—though his escort was not so pleased by the way hundreds of people crowded round to see this unexpected visitor—the prince rode away, by way of Mortehoe, to Barnstaple. He lunched at the *Fortescue* hotel, where he 'chatted and appeared quite to enjoy himself, expressing himself particularly pleased with the famous Devonshire cream and a luxurious apple tart served to him by his hostess'. After this, he caught the afternoon train to London, probably leaving north Devon buzzing with the excitement of having entertained a future king of England, though no doubt nonplussed by the brevity of his visit. A booklet produced by the Town Committee more than 30 years later ('Ilfracombe, a Resort for all Seasons of the Year') recorded that 'up to very recently Bobby, the pony on which his Royal Highness rode, was a curiosity that all visitors wished to see and most to mount . . . his death deprived Ilfracombe of an attraction to its visitors and a large income to its owner'.

The 1850s saw the establishment of two weekly newspapers in both of which newly-arrived holiday-makers could have the satisfaction of seeing their names printed. The *Ilfracombe Gazette, Arrival List and General Advertiser* was brought out by John Banfield in 1854, and four years later a rival bookseller, J. P. Bright, began to publish the *Ilfracombe Chronicle, North Devon News and Visitors' List.* (Bright also produced an eight-sheet paper called *Bright's Intelligencer and Arrival List* from June 1860 to May 1861.)

To Thomas Stabb and his like-minded associates, it was desirable that people—moneyed people, that is—should be encouraged not merely to visit Ilfracombe, but to settle there; from now on the shape, appearance and character of the town was largely decided by the speculative builder, encouraged by the local Board of Health. In 1856 Hostle Park estate was sold, and villas began to fill the open spaces on the hillside below Highfield Road, the former Sandy Lane. Daniel Benham, enjoying a walk along Sandy Lane in 1852, had referred to it as a pretty green lane, but to a local paper it was an 'old, narrow, dirty, impassable gorge behind this town, which in ancient times might have been called a road'. This was now widened, filled up, levelled 'and reduced to a civilised condition'; on Whit Monday, 1854, it was opened with what was described as a popular *fête champetre.* Like the Capstone Parade, it had been carried out with contributions from gentry and the more affluent townspeople as a winter scheme 'with the double view of finding employment for a number of necessitous labouring men out of work and preparing further promenading space for the public over ground affording some of the most splendid views of sea and cliff scenery anywhere to be obtained'. But if a gain in promenading space was one ostensible reason, it seems probable that an underlying one was the acquisition of a road that could be, and soon was, lined with more houses.

By no means all the residents in the town approved the changes going on, or the increase in the number of visitors. Kingsley's sister, Charlotte, the vicar's wife, probably expressed the opinion of a number of them in her book, *Ferny Combes,* published in 1857. (It may have been the popularity of her book that led John Dadds to establish a fernery at the foot of Langleigh Lane, which flourished until nearly the end of Victoria's reign.[5]) She would not try to describe a town, she said, where 'steam boats, coaches and vans do congregate, and where "parties", mounted on scraggy donkeys (looking as if they were allotted a straw per day) meet you at every turn'. She went on to say, with irony, that 'Ilfracombe is a pretty place, "a nice place", an agreeable place, a gay place, for it has a delightful public walk, terraced along the rocks, where a band plays twice a day, and folks walk up and down admiring the scenery and themselves; to say nothing of the soirees and public balls'.

On the Tunnels beach, 'one day last summer, we counted no less than 35 of those novel brown mushrooms, who have for the last two years infested the sea coast, all seated together so close that you could not have passed between them; besides sundry other specimens, in groups of half a dozen, some perched upon the rocks, some sketching, some making holes in muslin, others again diving into rock pools after unfortunate anemones, which, when touched, spouted out the water they had been leisurely imbibing, and drew in their pretty tentacles as rude hands detached them from their beloved rocks to be deposited in tumblers, there to be examined, tormented, and finally thrown out lifeless and decayed'.

The 'novel brown mushrooms' were, of course, women's hats, given the name because of their shape, that became fashionable as summer wear in the mid–19th century. Limpet hats were evidently another name for them; these are referred to in a short-lived periodical, *The Pixie, or, the Ilfracombe New Monthly Magazine, a Journal of Art, Nature and Human Nature,* of which the Revd. Chanter's two lively young curates, George Tugwell and Thomas Ravenshaw, brought out six monthly numbers in 1857. Ravenshaw described the Capstone with an almost Dickensian relish: 'Limpet hats with ladies young and old thereto attached; bluff slippers and telescopes with old gentlemen appended; sickly parsons with limp wives; noisy schoolboys luxuriating in midsummer holidays; and noisier children with frantic nurses; curs of every conceivable degree of ugliness and snappishness; donkeys and donkey drivers; wheel chairs and gasping propellors thereof; strange working men in odd caps and black satin scarves, with a strong development of hair under the chin, all smacking strongly of Bristol shops; a large party of Cambridge men supposed to be reading with a "coach", all apparently gifted with the art of colouring clay pipes to perfection; a few Oxonians, quiet, supercilious and neat, condemned as "muffs" by the more vivacious members of the sister University . . .'. (Evidently Ilfracombe remained popular as a place for undergraduate reading parties in the Long Vacation, 40 years after Fanny Burney had acted as anxious Flapper to her son, Alexander.)

George Tugwell[6] was an Oxford man himself, having taken his degree at Oriel College in 1852. His *A Manual of the Sea Anemones commonly found on the English Coast,* published in 1856, may have had something to do with the craze for collecting, and thus killing, the unfortunate sea anemones, but even more influential was a book that appeared three years earlier, Philip Gosse's *A Naturalist's Rambles on the Devonshire Coast.*[7]

Gosse was later to write a standard work, *The History of the British Sea Anemones and Corals.* His reputation as a zoologist stood high in mid-Victorian Britain—at least until his total opposition to the Darwinian theory of evolution made him appear ridiculous in the eyes of many fellow scientists. Today he is perhaps remembered chiefly because of that remarkable book, *Father and Son,* written by his only child, the biographer, linguist and critic, Sir Edmund Gosse, to whom his father's intense and narrow religious beliefs, as a member of the Plymouth Brethren, caused considerable oppression in his boyhood.

A Naturalist's Rambles is presented to readers as 'a mirror of the thoughts and feelings that have occupied my mind during a nine months' residence on the charming shores of North and South Devon'. Gosse, like Kingsley, was in search of better health; his doctor had advised a country holiday. He chose south Devon first, but after two months decided that it was not bracing enough, and moved himself, his wife and small son—then 'a little naturalist in petticoats', aged three—to Ilfracombe, where they stayed in a lodging house owned by a Mrs. Williams of Northfield. Gosse paid her a grateful tribute in a footnote to his book: 'We remained here the whole time of our residence in the place, six months; and during this period the unvarying cheerfulness and kindliness, the utter disregard of self, and the entire devotedness to our wishes, manifested by the inmates, were such as one rarely finds except from the warmest friends'.

His study looked out on the Baths and 'one or two pretty villas, with the fields of the Runnacleave behind them most richly green, sloping upwards to the edge of the cliffs that border the sea. The sheep, peacefully lying or grazing, speckle with white these verdant slopes; and young ladies come out there in the afternoon from one of the houses, with their targets and bows, to practise archery'.

Behind the house was a small grass plot which was at first bright with daisies and dandelions. The ripe seeds of the latter brought flocks of goldfinches, chaffinches and what Gosse spells Yellow *A*mmers to feed—until someone tidily mowed the grass and, to his regret, the birds came no more.

Referring to himself as, not a marine biologist, but a 'littoral naturalist', he devoted his days to the study that gave him constant and reverent joy: watching, dissecting or drawing molluscs and anelids, crustaceae, polyzoa and other organisms found between the tides: every one, to him, a living revelation of the benevolence of a personal Creator. His book is illustrated with his own delicate sketches and lithographs of these creatures, most of them made with the help of a microscope.

21. The north side of the Capstone in 1864, looking east, from Gadsby.

Botany, too, was a pleasure; walking over the slopes of Hillsborough—which he called a 'noble mountain-mass'—he noted rest-harrow, centaury, hawkweeds, thyme, Ladies' Bedstraw, bladder campion, varieties of stonecrop and bird's-foot trefoil. From the summit he looked down on Hele, seeing it 'embosomed in gardens and orchards, and half-hidden by tall and shaggy elms'—a beauty unimaginable today.

He made expeditions to all the places around Ilfracombe that have been known to visitors since it first became a summer resort, and intersperses his scientific descriptions of marine specimens with his impressions of Watermouth, Braunton and its Burrows, Lee, Woolacombe, Mortehoe and Bull Point. He climbed the Cairn—calling it Carn Top, as most people did in the 19th century— and walked over the Torrs. On a paddle-steamer voyage from Bristol, in late evening on a fine day, he watched the phosphorescence; 'as the vessel's bow sploughed (*sic*) up the water and threw off the liquid furrow on each side, brighter specks were left adhering to the dark planks, as the water fell off, and shone brilliantly until the next plunge washed them away. The foaming wash of the furrow itself was turbid with milky light, in which glowed spangles of intense brightness'. Most beautiful of all was the effect of the little waves driven forward by the paddle boxes, their curling glassy edges gleaming with a bluish light 'of the most vivid lustre, so intense that I could *almost* read the small print of a book that I held up over the gangway'.

22. The north side of the Capstone in 1864, looking west, from Gadsby.

And the glimpses he gives of mid-summer life in Ilfracombe's harbour are as lively as Fanny Burney's 35 years earlier. He liked to stand in the quiet lane above the ship-builder's yard, especially when fishing boats had just come in, the Bristol steamer was blowing off steam at the pier head, coasting schooners were taking on or discharging cargo, and pleasure skiffs full of 'laughing ladies and attentive beaux' were setting out to sail along the coast.

Crowds thronged the slopes of the Capstone, or climbed down to sit on ledges on the north side 'favourite spots with the ladies, who . . . seat themselves with their books or their netting on the little rocky perches by the hour together', or climbed the rocks of Wildersmouth to 'sit or lie at length in the pleasant sun, tempered by the breeze of summer'.

His religious beliefs made him severe about Lantern Hill, 'crowned with an ancient building that was once a Popish mass house, helping to diffuse spiritual darkness, but now makes some amends by exhibiting a nightly light to guide mariners to the harbour mouth'. (He was probably unaware that it had exhibited a nightly light, at least in winter, during the centuries when it *was* a 'Popish mass house'.)

Not only did he study sea anemones: finding them recommended as a delicacy by a French naturalist, he decided to cook some of the daisy anemony, *actinia crassicornis*. After a few attempts he tasted one, and invited his wife to join him. She was unable to swallow her portion, but their small son 'voted that "'tinny was good" and that "he liked 'tinny" and loudly demanded more, like another Oliver Twist'. Although this first experiment resulted in a dish he enjoyed, 'somewhat like the soft parts of a crab', which he ate with a sauce of vinegar, mustard, salt and pepper, he later fried some in egg and breadcrumbs, 'and they were very far superior to even the best on the former occasion'.

It was partly Gosse's book, and partly Tugwell's, that brought to Ilfracombe, in 1856, two writers of very dissimilar talents: Mary Ann Evans, who was soon to become widely known as George Eliot, and the man with whom she had begun to live in the previous year, and with whom she was to stay until he died (she outlived him by less than two years).

In fact, Ilfracombe very nearly saw the beginning of George Eliot's creativity as a novelist (she was already a practised literary journalist, working for the *Westminster Review*). In her reminiscences, 'How I came to write fiction', written at Richmond in December 1857, George Eliot recalled that September 1856 'made a new era in my life, for it was then I began to write Fiction'. Very soon after she and Lewes crossed the Bristol Channel, in one of the regular steam packets, to Tenby (which seemed 'tame and vulgar' after Ilfracombe), she lay in bed one morning 'thinking what should be the subject of my first story'. Her thoughts merged into a dreamy doze, and she imagined herself writing a story with the title *The Sad Fortunes of the Reverend Amos Barton*. She told Lewes, who exclaimed 'Oh what a capital title!' From that moment she settled in her mind that this should be her first story.

Lewes was writing a series of *Seaside Studies,* followed closely in the footsteps of Gosse, for *Blackwood's Magazine,* and it was in Blackwood's that the first three stories by George Eliot that make up *Scenes from Clerical Life* were to appear, Lewes negotiating the acceptance on behalf of his anonymous friend. (There was at first no suspicion that the author was a woman: it was thought that the stories were the work of a cleric, probably a Cambridge man.)

The couple had arrived in Ilfracombe by train from London to Barnstaple (breaking the journey at Exeter overnight) and then by 'the good old-fashioned stage coach', which put them down at the *Clarence* hotel. Looking for lodgings, they first tried Mrs. Williams, so enthusiastically recommended by Gosse, but were not attracted by her 'shabby ill-furnished parlour and bedroom'. However, 'At this spot, called Northfield, the beauty of Ilfracombe burst upon us, though we had as yet no glimpse of the sea and no idea—at least *I* had none—in which direction it lay. On our left were gracefully sloping green hills, on our right the clustering houses and beyond, hills with bold, rocky sides'.

They came upon the house Fanny Kingsley had approved, Runnymede Villa. Although they feared at first glance that it might be too smart and expensive, they were delighted to find that they could have a large double drawing room, with bedroom and dressing room above, for a guinea a week during May and one and a half guineas in June.

23. Hele, near Ilfracombe, as Philip Gosse saw it in 1853, 'embosomed in gardens and orchards, and half-hidden by tall and shaggy elms'.

They soon began to search the rock pools for zoophytes. Some tall glass jars they had brought with them turned out to be unsuitable for keeping their discoveries. Lewes called on Mr. Tugwell—then 26 years old—and found him 'a very nice little fellow'. (In a letter George Eliot speaks of him as 'a charming little zoological curate, who is a delightful companion on expeditions and is most good-natured in lending and giving apparatus and "critturs" of all sorts'.) Yellow pie dishes, they found, were the best artificial habitat for *actiniae*. In a 'quiet little nook at the back of the dissenting chapel opposite Wildersmouth' was a shop kept by a Mr. Hele, who collected marine animals and sold them to a shop near Regent's Park that supplied London naturalists, and there they saw many specimens that fascinated them.

24. The beach at Lee, west of Ilfracombe, in 1860, from Gadsby. To George Eliot, the village of Lee seemed to have lodged itself 'like a tiny colony of *Aurora Actiniae*, in the nick between two ranges of hills'.

Walking inland or along the coast, they were constantly enchanted by the beauty of everything they saw, 'the graceful green Capstone Hill, surmounted by its Flagstaff' and 'Hillsborough with its crag of rich, violet-veiled brown' with, farther away, 'the sombre Hangman' lifting its round, blackened shoulder. The Torrs, which they only visited once (there was an admission charge of threepence, and they were economising so strictly that they 'could not afford a sixpenny walk very frequently') reminded George Eliot of 'some noble animal that has reared itself on its forelegs to look at something, powerfully arresting its attention—as if the land had lifted itself up in amazed contemplation of the glorious sea'. This sentence, incidentally, like many of George Eliot's descriptions of scenery around Ilfracombe, was incorporated by Lewes in *Seaside Studies*.

With her recent marine studies in mind, Lee seemed to her to have lodged itself 'like a tiny colony of *Aurora Actiniae*, in the nick between two ranges of hills'; it had an ornamental cottage or two as well as genuine cottages, and by the side of the road was the little Gothic chapel 'where our nice Mr. Tugwell preaches every Sunday'. (In 1869, Tugwell was to become the first incumbent of the new ecclesiastical parish of Lee.) The great charm of the road to Lee, as of all Devonshire lanes, she thought, was 'the springs you detect gushing in shady recesses covered with liverwort, with here and there waving tufts of fern and other broad-leaved plants that love obscurity and moisture. Springs are sacred places still for those who love and reverence Nature'.

On their way to Chambercombe they passed through a farm that had by its gate 'a perfect miniature of some Swiss "Falls"'. Here cows stared at them 'with formidable timidity, such as I have sometimes seen in a human being who frightens others while he is frightened himself'. There was a wide place in the lane where several gates opened and wild flowers were unusually luxuriant; a few rough trunks lay against tufts of fern and a quiet donkey grazed against a background of steep hill, half orchard and half grass. Farther on 'a great awkward puppy always came flopping after them' in another small farm yard belonging to a small shabby house with broken windows stuffed with rags. This, she says, was known as the Haunted House—but as it does not sound like Chambercombe Manor, possibly she has confused the latter's ghost story with this smaller house. Near this place they liked to sit down to rest and look at the sunlight 'living like a spirit among the branches of the hanging woods'.

Despite her initial delight, at Northfield, in the beauty of Ilfracombe, it was evidently the surroundings of the town that had pleased her. As bricks and mortar it had no charm, she thought; the new terraces, so much admired by writers of guide books, only made her think of 'two factory-like lines of buildings on the slopes of a green hill'. Yet even these could be improved by certain lights: one evening, after a shower, 'as the sun was setting over the sea behind us, some peculiar arrangement of clouds threw a delicious evening light on the irregular cluster of houses and merged the ugliness of their forms in an exquisite flood of colour . . . A perfect rainbow arched over the picture'.

Ilfracombe was already being visited by one of the German bands that were a feature of so many seaside places in Victorian England. According to Lewes, this one played daily, for six weeks, just four tunes' 'Partant pour le Syrie'. 'The Low-backed Car', 'The Red and the Blue' and 'God Save the Queen', never anything else and always pitilessly out of tune.

The ratification of the peace with Russia that ended the Crimean War was celebrated on 29 May 1856. A tea was provided for working people in the High Street; there were races for boys; bonfires on Hillsborough and the Torrs; and 'some feeble fireworks on the Capstone'. A very small procession—no more than four or five men in miscellaneous uniforms, George Eliot said—'mounted on Rosinantes' paraded through the town; she supposed that they were meant to represent the Allied armies.

One evening, hearing a 'choral howl', she and Lewes went out to find three itinerant preachers on the Quay, their audience a group of fishermen who listened in respectful silence, though boys and girls jeered, laughed, and beat tin kettles. A young man stood on a chair and preached Mormonism, flinging his arms about. Lewes found him distressing to listen to, but the only criticism he heard came from a grey-haired fisherman who observed 'He doesn't speak according to Scripter'.

Like Fanny Burney, though unlike Gosse and Kingsley, they considered Ilfracombe's air too harsh. It was not a favourable place, George Eliot wrote to a friend, for delicate people: 'Mr. Lewes has felt so poorly for the last week that we think of going elsewhere'. In view of this, it seems surprising that they chose to go farther north, to Tenby.

On the last night of their stay, George Tugwell visited them, and they had music until eleven o'clock, 'a pleasant recollection'. Later, George Eliot was to recall that 'Mr. Tugwell's acquaintance was a real acquisition to us, not only because he was a companion and helper in zoological pursuits, but because to know him was to know of another sweet nature in the world. It is always good to know, if only in passing, a charming human being—it refreshes one like flowers, and woods and clear brooks'.

Chapter Ten

VICTORIAN ADVANCEMENTS

FOR MANY YEARS of the 19th century, the remnants of one of Ilfracombe's two medieval manors were in the possession of Sir Bourchier Palk Wrey, descendant of the Fitzwarrens. The 1839 tithe map shows that his property included Capstone, Compass and Lantern Hills, the harbour and its pier and shipyard, Quayfield House and Castle House, the Town Pound, and some 100 houses in the harbour area. The other manor, Saxon in origin, and taken over by the Norman family of Champernowne after the Conquest, no longer existed; its last owner, Richard, Lord Gorges, Baron of Dundalk, had sold it off in several lots in the late 17th century; in 1678 he reserved in trust 'the Land and Tenements of the Ropers for ever, for the benefit of the Minister', according to the terrier of 1745.

The main aim of influential local people, including Sir Bourchier himself, was to continue the rate of building as steadily as possible, still hoping to bring about an imitation Brighton. Yet the ancient ritual of the manorial court-leet still exerted a fascination, and Sir Bourchier evidently enjoyed exercising this right.

The last one of which, it seems, a record exists, was reported in the *North Devon Journal* for 16 December 1858. The court met at 11 a.m. at the *Britannia* hotel, and a jury of 12 men, every one of them a master mariner, was sworn in. (The foreman, Charles Dennis, no longer went to sea; one of Sir Bourchier's principal tenants, he now ran the shipyard, and was the builder of the two largest vessels every produced there, the *Kossuth* and the *Coronella*.) The Portreeve, James Camp, the harbour-master, and representatives of a firm of solicitors with branches in Ilfracombe and Barnstaple were also present.

'Though a far less important matter than formerly, and the court not so frequently held, yet it is not without its use . . . and from its great antiquity, as a relict of the feudal ages, and as a last depository of the local customs and traditions, it is not wanting in interest', the *Journal* observed.

The jury made a tour of inspection of the harbour, Compass Hill and Lantern Hill, where the lighthouse keeper, John Davie, 'the careful keeper of that important pharos', was evidently doing his job well: lantern, reflectors and everything to do with the maintenance of the light were in excellent order. (John Davie was to continue to live in the little chapel, where he and his wife brought up 13 children, until 1871, when blasting operations connected with the building of the new promenade pier forced them to leave.) Having made some recommendations concerning safety posts and chains around the harbour, into which a coastguard had recently contrived to fall one dark night, and sorted out a couple of minor disputes about property, the jury returned to the *Britannia* 'led by the foreman who, finding himself at the head of so respectable a following, came down Fore Street in due state, the market people looking at them with reverent regard, taking them for a company returning from a funeral'.

They were joined by Mr. Scamp, the town crier, and sat down at three o'clock to what was perhaps the main business of the day: a 'sumptuous repast', after which toasts were drunk 'with the greatest enthusiasm' and speeches made.[1] Sir Bourchier declared that some of his earliest and happiest memories were connected with Ilfracombe; he assured the company that whatever promoted its extension, prosperity and advancement would always give him pleasure.

A convinced Liberal in politics, Deputy Lieutenant of Devon and a J.P., Sir Bourchier was the eighth holder of what was then one of the oldest existing baronetages; the title had been created in 1628, its first holder being Sir Chichester Wrey of Trebitch in Cornwall. (According to Debrett, the family of Wrey was supposed by Wotton to be descended from Robert le Wrey, who lived at the time of King Stephen.) In 1652 Sir Chichester married Lady Anne Bourchier, a daughter of the fourth Earl of Bath, and so became the owner of Tawstock Court, the home of the Bourchiers for centuries. The eighth baronet added 'Palk' to his name because his mother was a daughter of Sir Robert Palk of Halsdon House; after her death his father married again and had a daughter and a son, and it was the latter, the Rev. Henry Bourchier Wrey, who succeeded to the baronetcy in 1879, as Sir Bourchier had only three daughters, all of whom predeceased him.

Like his father, Sir Bourchier married twice. His first wife was an Irish widow, Mrs. Riddle, a Roman Catholic. Having inherited Tawstock Court in 1826, at the age of 38, he lived there until his eldest daughter married Edward Weld of Lulworth Castle; he then lent the house to the young couple and moved to Ilfracombe. When Weld eventually inherited Lulworth, Tawstock was leased to a G. H. Pinckney for many years. The lease having expired, Sir Bourchier thought of returning to end his days in his ancestral home, but perhaps he was by then too old and too firmly attached to Ilfracombe to endure a move.

Most of the above biographical details are taken from his obituary in the *North Devon Journal,* the tone of which indicates that his marriage, and his later conversion to his wife's faith, caused some scandal in an area as stoutly Protestant as north Devon. (The *Western Times* went so far as to say that his first marriage 'had set a dark shadow on the place'.) For her sake he had an oratory constructed in Tawstock House, established a Roman Catholic chaplain there and, a year after her death in 1842, fulfilled a promise he had made to her by building a Roman Catholic church, priest's house and school in Barnstaple, on a site he had bought for £160. Not many years before his own death he bought Trafalgar House in Broad Street, Ilfracombe,[2] and presented it for use as a Roman Catholic chapel, Our Lady Star of the Sea. (The present Roman Catholic church is in Runnacleave Road.)

Sir Bourchier's second wife, by whom he had no children, was a Miss Eliza Coles of Tawstock; she, too, died before him.

It is usually accepted that Quayfield House, on the south side of the harbour, was built in the early 18th century, when the 6th baronet was lord of the manor of Ilfracombe. The obituary, however, remarks that 'Lady Bourchier died in the same house (which she had built for herself in the event of her outliving Sir Bourchier) in which her husband has now deceased after an interval of 38 years'— and Sir Bourchier died in Quayfield House.

An aquatint of the harbour of 1814 certainly shows no house in the position of the present Quayfield House, although it depicts one on the hillside slightly to the east.

Although he said that he was ready to do 'anything in his power to promote the enlargement of Ilfracombe', he saw that this did not necessarily mean building on every part of it. For this reason he sold the Capstone to the local Board of Health for £2,500, two years before he died; he wanted it to remain the town's property for ever, and 'when it was feared that parts of it might be built upon, he expressed his anxiety that it should be preserved for public recreation'.

Whereas, in 1828, Ilfracombe had seemed to Thomas Cornish the Brighton of Barnstaple and the north of Devon, it was now the declared aim of a local group of entrepreneurs to make it 'the Brighton of the South West'. They formed the Ilfracombe Joint Stock Land and Investment Company in 1860 with a view to covering the northern side of the valley of the West Wilder Brook, running under the magnificent slopes of the Torrs, with what were described as luxury villas. The villas may have been profitable to the members of the Torrs Park Company, as it was usually known, but they were over-ambitious in size; rising four or five storeys under their steeply-pitched slate roofs, they epitomised a High Victorian confidence in ample incomes and an unlimited supply of servants content with small wages; within a few decades several were being converted into schools and hotels. (Among the schools were the Ilfracombe College, Ilfracombe Ladies' College, and Hereford House School, which occupied two houses; a little later a Convent School of the Immaculate Conception was opened.)[3]

After luxury villas, a luxury hotel. A consortium was set up, the Ilfracombe Hotel and Esplanade Company (the ubiquitous Thomas Stabb was a member of both this and of the Torrs Park Company); the chairman was Thomas Fry, a leading figure among those working to ensure that the railway reached the town as soon as possible. A sea-front site overlooking Wildersmouth and the Capstone was obtained, and building began.

When the hotel was opened on 15 May 1867, the local paper observed that 'Ilfracombe has been emulating her sister watering places . . . and now boasts of a building which for size, sumptuousness and convenience of arrangement is not surpassed by any of the monster hotels in the kingdom . . . She now holds high rank among our fashionable sea-side resorts'.

The building, of coloured bricks, was 150 feet in length. It had been designed 'in the French Gothic style' by M. C. W. Horne, a London architect, and built by contractors from Plymouth. Its status as an absolutely up-to-the-minute establishment was proved by the fact that when you walked into its entrance hall, one of the first things you noticed was a telegraph office. There were 210 rooms, including a smoking room and a library and reading room. Segregation of the sexes seems to have been aimed for much of the time: there was a ladies' coffee room, a ladies' dining-room, and a ladies' drawing-room.

A number of bedrooms were set aside for visitors' servants (1s. 6d. a night; day board, 4s.). Single rooms for guests cost from 1s. 6d. to 5s.; double rooms, 4s. to 6s. Baths might cost 6d., 1s. or 2s., but on what principle the prices varied (depth? temperature?) is not explained. Dinner cost 3s. 6d., and four types of breakfast were available: plain, meat, *table d'hote,* and ham and eggs.

25.   Ilfracombe as it appeared in about 1870 to an observer looking down from the Torrs. Both the *Ilfracombe Hotel* and some of the new houses in Torrs Park Road may be seen.

Each morning, Sundays excepted, an express four-horse omnibus left the hotel at 9 a.m. for Barnstaple railway station; it returned at 5.30 p.m. on the arrival of the express from London. Advertisements announced that the hotel 'stands in its own ornamental grounds, five acres in extent, and a private terrace on the north side, nearly one thousand feet in length, affords the finest marine promenade attached to any hotel in the United Kingdom. The newly-constructed walks overlook the bright clear water of the Bristol Channel and command extensive views of beautiful coast scenery. Good stabling and lock-up Coach House. Post horses and carriages always ready. Sailing boats and yachts also provided'.

At the same time the *Royal Britannia* ('Royal' since the Prince of Wales's visit in 1856) which was also owned by the Ilfracombe Hotel and Esplanade Company, had been redecorated and refurnished; it offered accommodation at lower terms for those whose tastes were less luxurious or whose means were more modest.

The *Ilfracombe* hotel was an immediate success, so much so that a new wing was added within a few years. The directors also had plans to acquire part of the remainder of Ropery Meadow on which to build an aquarium, winter garden, skating rink, and assembly or concert hall, and the Local Board was willing to let them the land for 999 years 'subject to the written consent of the General Board', but either the latter refused permission or the project appeared too expensive. It was to be 1888 before a winter garden, doubling as a concert hall, without skating rink, but with a small aquarium, was built.

The hotel was particularly pleased to welcome, in September 1878, one of Queen Victoria's grandsons, Prince Frederick William of Prussia. The future Kaiser was then a young man of not quite twenty. He travelled incognito, as Count von Valingen, from Waterloo Station, with a large retinue. During his fortnight's stay, according to the *North Devon Herald,* he visited Mortehoe to watch the quarterly exercise of the lifeboat, *Grace Woodbury.* The villagers erected a decorated arch in his honour, and turned out in force to welcome him. In Ilfracombe he 'appeared frequently in the public walks' and 'liberally patronised boating', taking care to hire all the boatmen in turn. On Sundays he attended the parish church, where the Bishop of Oxford preached. He was an early riser, often bathing from Rapparee beach between six and seven in the morning. On his departure he told the manager of the *Ilfracombe* hotel how pleased he had been with his accommodation. Catching a train back to Waterloo, he then travelled on to Balmoral to join the royal family.

One incident, hushed up during his stay, was given a great deal of publicity more than 30 years later. The bathing huts at Rapparee were owned by a boatman named Price. One morning when Price's son, Alfred, a young man in his twenties, was in charge of the huts, Prince Frederick, apparently bored, began to throw stones at them, and took no notice when asked to stop. Alfred tried to prevent him forcibly, and a fight began in which the prince was getting the worst of it when some of his entourage arrived and intervened.

According to a paper read to the Ilfracombe Rotary Club in 1928 by the Revd. W. Joyce, rector of Charles, 'Price was known to the end of his life as "the man who fought the Kaiser"'. This may be regarded as an overstatement: Prince Frederick did not become Kaiser until 1888, and to the British public in general did not become an object of distrust and dislike until his militarism and territorial ambition began to seem actively threatening in the early 1900s. But it was natural that once the First World War broke out, Alfred Price should become a local hero, especially as a set of doggerel verses celebrating his fight on Rapparee was published in the town.[4] He died in 1923, five years after the ex-Kaiser had retired to Holland.

Mr. Joyce goes into considerable detail about one of the members of Prince Frederick's retinue, Count von Hackburg, who, he says, settled in a large house on Exmoor overlooking the Bristol Channel, became a district councillor, churchwarden and magistrate, and used this respectable façade to work as a German spy. He frequently received German guests; among them, local people claimed to recognise the Kaiser. Moreover, one day in 1911, Alfred Price, working aboard the paddle steamer *Lorna Doone,* was convinced that one of the passengers, whose name, he discovered, was given as Count von Valingen, was the man he had fought in 1878.

Possibly it was with a view to avoiding any further such contretemps for their guests that, notwithstanding the convenient nearness of both the hot and cold baths and the Tunnel beaches, the directors of the *Ilfracombe* hotel ordered the building of covered baths, 160 feet by 50 feet, to be filled with sea water by a steam pump. Sixty dressing rooms were provided. The baths were open daily from 7 a.m. to 7 p.m., and were reserved for ladies from 10 a.m. to 2 p.m.

Swimming instructors were employed; the swimming master, as he was called, was always referred to as 'Professor' Parker; the swimming mistress was a Miss McGarrick. They did not merely teach swimming; they often gave displays, which were reported in the local press. R. D. Blackmore, the author of *Lorna Doone,*

26.   A view of the town from the Capstone in 1864 with the *Ilfracombe Hotel* in the right foreground. (From Gadsby.)

was present at one of these, and watched while 'a male and female professor of the natatory art took afternoon tea at a table floating in the middle of the water with rather more grace than many people display in a drawing room. The male professor, indeed, seemed more at home in the water than out of it, and did all kinds of wonderful things, under the inspiring strains of a brass band'. (According to Lilian Wilson, in her *Ilfracombe's Yesterdays*, Professor Parker would also give 'excellent displays of fancy diving' from the centre of the pier when the tide was high.)

One building that Ilfracombe lacked was a hospital (although the tithe apportionment of 1839 shows that Charles Dennis, the shipbuilder, was trustee of a Sailors' Hospital.) Mrs. Anne Tyrrell decided in 1864 to provide two beds in a cottage in Horne Lane as an experiment. According to Morris's *Directory for Devon* of 1870, her purpose was 'to see whether it would be a benefit to the poor, and if the expense could be brought within reasonable limits. The demand for more beds and accommodation having become greater, it was found necessary to erect a building for that purpose, and on 27 August 1868 the first stone of the present edifice was laid by its original founder at Higher Horne'.

27. The new promenade pier, completed in 1873, the year before
this drawing was published. (From Gadsby.)

When the hospital was opened two years later, no fewer than five members of the clergy, including the Revd. Tyrrell and the Revd. John Mill Chanter, attended a special service 'compiled for the occasion' and held on the site. (As one of the two medical officers appointed, Thomas Stabb was present.) The cost of the building was estimated at £1,000; it was to have a special ward for convalescents and to be 'replete with all modern improvements'. Although it opened with only six beds, the Tyrrell Cottage Hospital was enlarged in 1896 to provide 25 beds; however, as an advertisement in the *Ilfracombe Gazette* observed, the following year, 'the endowment is very small, and subscriptions and donations are much needed'. It was open to visitors on Mondays, Tuesdays and Fridays from 2 to 4 p.m., and it was evidently hoped that such visitors would not forget the collection box at the end of their tour. A Hospital Saturday Fund had been set up not long after it opened, and its flag day, held annually in August, usually brought in about £250 in the 1890s and early 1900s.

Care of another sort, for the saving of life at sea, was advanced in 1866 when the Ilfracombe lifeboat station was formally taken over by the Royal National Lifeboat Institution, and a new lifeboat, the *Broadwater,* was provided. As early as 1815 the customs officer at Ilfracombe, Thomas Rodd, had suggested that a lifeboat should be available in the harbour; a number of English coastal towns, including Plymouth and Exmouth, already had such boats. And although his idea was not, it seems, taken up immediately, the Lysons' *Magna Britannia,* published in 1822, noted that 'Three large skiffs cruise here in the winter season for the express purpose of assisting vessels in distress'. Four years after the founding, in 1824, of the R.N.L.I., the town received its first official lifeboat, a pilot gig 'fitted up for life-saving on what was known as the Palmer plan designed by George Palmer, Deputy Chairman of the R.N.L.I.'.[5] Her name and service records are unknown. Local tradition said that her successor was presented by the explorer, Sir John Franklin, in 1850, and named after his wife; however, Grahame Farr, in his detailed account of Ilfracombe lifeboats, shows that this is unlikely.[6]

Reliable records begin with the *Broadwater.* She was the gift of a Londoner, Robert Broadwater. Built on the Thames, she was of the standard self-righting type of her time, 32 feet long and rowed by 10 oars. Her launching was celebrated with all the usual ceremony so beloved of the 19th century. Mounted on a transporting carriage drawn by six grey horses and manned by her crew, she was escorted in a lengthy procession from Hillsborough Terrace to the harbour; the bands of the 6th and 21st Devon Rifle Volunteers played, the route was lined with spectators, and when Lord Fortescue had made a speech, Lady Fortescue named the boat, which was launched to cheering and the booming of cannon.[7]

The *Broadwater* was to save 45 lives during her years at Ilfracombe. Not many months after her arrival she went to the assistance of an American full-rigged ship in danger off Morte, and having taken off the captain's wife and children—lowered to her in a basket—and delivered them safely to Ilfracombe, went back and stood by all night until the storm eased and the ship could be towed across the Bristol Channel to Cardiff.

Until this time, a lifeboat house had stood on part of the site of the present Hierns Lane. To shelter the *Broadwater,* a new boathouse was built at the foot of Lantern Hill, and a slipway at Warphouse Point was used to launch her. With the building of the promenade pier, this was no longer possible; for more than 100 years, Ilfracombe's lifeboat had to be towed along the Quay, round to the harbour by way of Broad Street, and into the water until, according to the state of the tide, she floated free. (In 1983 the present lifeboat, the *Lloyds II,* was

1. Sir Bourchier Palk Wrey (a descendant of the Bourchiers, Barons Fitzwarren, who held the harbour manor for centuries) and his second wife standing near the ancient Warp House. As Sir Bourchier does not appear old in this picture, it must date from the very early days of photography: he died in 1879, aged 91.

2. (*right*) The coast to the west of Ilfracombe, showing the walks cut in the seaward slopes of the great seven-crested ridge of the Torrs that protects Ilfracombe from the north-west.

3. (*below*) The coast to the east of Ilfracombe. Along this road the four-horse excursion coaches regularly travelled to Lynton every summer from the 1870s until the First World War.

4. The harbour of Ilfracombe, probably about 1890, but although earlier ships would have been differently designed and rigged, and the houses on the Quay would have been smaller, a scene such as this would not have looked altogether strange to an observer standing on the Strand at any time from the 14th century onwards.

5. (*above*) This print is dated 1851 by the Ilfracombe Museum; the ship would therefore almost certainly have been the *Kossuth* (later re-named the *Maggie*) built by Charles Dennis and completed in 1852. The shipyard was on the south side of the harbour.

6. Rodney Lane, one of the narrow streets near the harbour which no longer exist. The pub was named in honour of Admiral Rodney, probably after the prize he sent back from the West Indies was wrecked off Hillsborough in 1792; the lane may have had an earlier name abandoned in favour of the admiral's.

7. The paddle steamers *Velindra* and *Eclair* lying off Warp House Point, probably some time in the 1860s, when passengers often had to be ferried to the steamers by boats.

8. Once the new pier was completed, as many as six paddle steamers could lie side by side, as this photograph shows, and people can still recall having to make their way across several ships when re-embarking. The paddle steamers here are *Bonnie Doone* (an accident-prone vessel nicknamed the 'Bonnie Break-doone' by a local wit), *Lorna Doone*, *Scotia*, *Britannia*, *Cambria* and *Brighton*.

9. (*above*) Larkstone beach in the late 19th century, after the building of the promenade pier which may be seen across the harbour. Limestone and coal are being unloaded to be burned in the limekiln not far from this beach. If present plans to use Larkstone as the landing place for a roll-on, roll-off ferry to South Wales are realised, the cove will inevitably become unrecognisable.

10. (*left*) Looking down on Rapparee beach with its line of bathing huts, much as they would have looked in 1878 when Alfred Price fought Prince Frederick Wilhelm of Prussia (later Kaiser Wilhelm II) for throwing stones at them.

11. (*below*) Some of the 'luxury villas' built in the 1860s along a road cut into the lower slopes of the Torrs (Torrs Park Road) which within a few decades became schools. From left to right: Ilfracombe College; the Convent School of the Immaculate Conception, opened in 1907; and two houses converted in the 1890s as Hereford House School for girls.

2. The front of the *Ilfracombe Hotel* as it appeared in the years after its opening in 1867.

3. The back of the *Ilfracombe Hotel*, showing its own swimming baths, built in 1880, and its private esplanade.

14. The glass and iron pavilion or winter garden, built in 1888 to celebrate Queen Victoria's Golden Jubilee, as it appeared until 1924, when its central section was demolished to make way for a theatre.

15. The interior of the Pavilion before 1924.

16. One of the 'Season Bands' that played every summer in the Pavilion and at the nearby bandstand.

17. The Pavilion Theatre, completed in 1925, and the bandstand.

18. The south side of the harbour at the beginning of this century. The buildings on the left were all demolished about 1907.

19. The Quay, with vehicles which may be cabs or early motor cars, parked outside the *Britannia Hotel*.

20. Where the east end of the High Street meets Fore Street and Portland Street. The fire of 1896 began in the building at the junction of these streets - then the property of Mr. Cole, an ironmonger and furniture dealer - and the flames were carried across the top of Fore Street to set the Arcade alight. In the fire of 1983 the Arcade was again burned out.

21. The High Street c. 1900, showing the raised bank, removed later in the century, and the rank for horse cabs beside it.

22. R. Martin, one of the best-known of Ilfracombe's Town Criers, a familiar figure in Edwardian days.

23. (*below*) Ketches on the Strand c. 1900, among them the *Kate*, built at Appledore in 1865.

24. Mr. Copp's coach *Alert* standing outside the little Greek Doric-style Baths built in 1836. Runnymede (or Runnamede) Villa, where Charles Kingsley and his family stayed in 1849, and where George Eliot and George Henry Lewes spent a few weeks in 1856, may be seen on the right of the picture.

25. The rival coach firm: Sam Colwill and his son Tom standing beside the white-ruffed child in the foreground. The team of three horses of differing colours suggests that this was a relief coach; Sam's four-horse teams of greys were locally famous. This photograph probably dates from about 1905.

26. (*above*) In August 1905, the *North Devon Journal* reported an excursion crowd of this sort. These are Lancashire mill workers on holiday in Ilfracombe in 1911.

27. (*left*) The Tunnels beach in the early 20th century. Mixed bathing was at last allowed there in 1905.

28. One of Ilfracombe's very old pubs, the *Golden Lion*, knocked down when the Quay was widened between 1893 and 1895.

29. A group of Ilfracombe boatmen in the days before a wall had been built along the Quay. Some were known by such nicknames as Sunshine Ley, Brown Jug Lovering, Tatty Bushen and Low Water Dick.

30. By the time this photograph was taken, perhaps in the 1890s, donkeys had been offered for hire to visitors for at least a century. In the late 19th century, a bye-law laid down 'one ass, not more than one passenger' for small vehicles of the sort that appears here.

31. Evidently Edwardian ladies rode side-saddle, even on donkeys. The summer season must have meant a hard life for the donkeys, in times when concern for animal welfare was less than it is today.

32. The harbour from Hillsborough in the days when paddle steamers visited regularly in summer. The steamers have already gone, and if plans put forward in 1983 for a floating harbour prove practicable, the whole area will be entirely changed.

moved from the pier boathouse for a few months, as people living along the Quay had complained that the noisy, heavy caterpillar tractor used to haul her launcher was undermining the foundations of their properties. A new rubber-wheeled tractor having been provided, the *Lloyds II* was returned to her home.)

As the number of passengers and pleasure steamers visiting Ilfracombe grew, the inconvenience of having no pier at which they could come alongside at any state of the tide became increasingly evident. Sir Bourchier Palk Wrey decided to continue family tradition by helping to make possible the building of such a pier. His father had begun the repair of the pier forming the inner harbour, and after his death Sir Bourchier himself had finished the work. To the 18th-century inscription that set out their ancestors' record of pier-building, he had added 'A further enlargement of this pier was commenced by Sir Bourchier Wrey, Bart., in the year 1824 and completed in the year 1829 by Sir Bourchier Palk Wrey, the present lord of the manor'.

Now, at the age of 82, an Act of Parliament having been obtained for widening the Quay and extending it to the end of Warphouse Point, he made himself and his successors responsible for a loan of £10,000, advanced by the Public Works Commissioners at a low rate of interest, to be repaid in 48 years. When the work was finished in 1874, it had taken longer than expected, but on 15 May the opening was celebrated with almost as much pomp and ceremony as had attended the Duchess of Clarence's visit, earlier in the century. Shops were closed, a procession marched round the town with bands playing, and passed under a triumphal arch erected outside the *Britannia* hotel that bore the words 'God Bless Sir Bourchier'. Bunting decorated ships in the harbour, and the lifeboat flew streamers on its carriage. Guns fired a salute; among them two old cannon that for years had purported to guard the harbour. These, unfortunately, burst, knocking a hole in the bottom of a boat, but no one was hurt.

Sir Bourchier, 85 by this time, climbed nimbly on to the roof of his carriage and made a speech, declaring that it was the proudest day of his life. The contractor, not to be outdone, climbed to the roof of *his* carriage and spoke at some length, referring to Sir Bourchier as 'the sole projector of the enterprise' and saying that Ilfracombe was lucky to have such a benefactor. Optimistically, he declared that there could be no rivalry or competition between the pier and the railway that was soon to reach the town: some visitors would arrive by sea and leave by train, and vice versa.

This was not an entirely mistaken prophecy; once the railway arrived, the following year, a fairly high proportion of the ever-increasing numbers of holiday-makers it was to bring to Ilfracombe during the next 80 years or so probably took trips along the coast, or across to Lundy, in one or other of the excursion steamers that made use of the new pier every summer.

The opening of the railway was indeed·an occasion of almost more fervent rejoicing than the opening of the pier. For 20 years, since the North Devon Railway had linked Barnstaple to Exeter, many people had worked to make possible a continuation to Ilfracombe, but difficulties over the choice of a suitable route, obtaining appropriate Acts of Parliament and raising money had caused delay after delay. One of the earliest enthusiasts for the scheme, an Exeter solicitor named Robert Wreford, died before the first navvies, wagons and horses arrived at Braunton in 1871 to begin work on the line. Although it was only a narrow gauge, single-line light railway (the Exeter to Barnstaple line was originally broad gauge and did not change to standard gauge until 1881; the Barnstaple to Ilfracombe section was not doubled until the late 1880s) the townspeople were jubilant. On 21 July 1874, the usual bands and processions, with almost the entire population either marching or looking on, passed under a succession of arches bearing such mottoes as 'Success to the Railway', 'Prosperity to the Town', 'United in Bands of Iron', 'Queen of the West', 'May the Rails of the New Line Never Rust', and 'Waterloo to Ilfracombe'. At last the link to the country-wide railway network, essential to a rising resort, had been achieved.

Chapter Eleven

BY RAIL, ROAD OR SEA

HOWEVER MUCH Sir Bourchier Wrey rejoiced in the extension and enlargement of Ilfracombe, and entrepreneurs and developers enjoyed the profits to be obtained from promoting it, there were those who were more inclined to agree with Gratiana, John Mill Chanter's daughter, who ended her *Wanderings in North Devon* (written in the 1880s) by dedicating the book to 'lovers of the beautiful place and its church . . . those who remember if fifty years ago, when meadows stretched from the church to the Quay, and the scythes clinked merrily in the early mornings when the hay harvest came, and when the *Mumpers'* inn and the stocks were places of importance. Where are the meadows and the winding pathways now? Ah where? where the landrails craiked in scores all through the summer nights, now bricks and mortar reign supreme'. (The landrails had been noticed by George Eliot and George Henry Lewes; he wrote that he had heard them perpetually, day and night, from the majestic Seven Torrs, their cry reminding him of the creaking of a wicker basket.)

One meadow was still an open space: Ropery Meadow, which the local Board of Health bought in 1882 for £2,203, to be used as a recreation ground, but it is probable that the only birds to be heard crying over it by then were herring gulls planing in from the sea, or the jackdaws that still find the slopes of the Capstone a good feeding ground.

It is to be regretted that an intelligent, observant girl who visited Ilfracombe twice, in 1882 and 1883, and who was to develop into one of the most talented and popular of all author-illustrators of books for children, did not leave us any description of the town as she saw it. One of her books begins: 'When I was a child I used to go to the seaside for the holidays. We stayed in a little town where there was a harbour and fishing boats and fishermen'. The little town is given the name Stymouth, and a number of different places provided aspects of it—Sidmouth, Teignmouth, Lyme Regis and Hastings. But like Ilfracombe, it contained a Broad Street and a Fore Street, and a short cut to the harbour down a steep flight of steps such as existed in Victorian Ilfracombe: steps that were 'too steep and slippery for anyone less sure-footed than a cat . . . rather dark and slimy, between high backs of houses. A smell of ropes and pitch and a good deal of noise came up from below. At the bottom of the steps was the quay, or landing place, beside the inner harbour', and when the tide was out, there was no water in that inner harbour, and the vessels rested 'on the dirty mud'. In her old age, when she had long ceased to write children's books, Beatrix Potter told an enquirer that Ilfracombe had given her the idea of the steps that are described in *The Tale of Little Pig Robinson*; she had written a draft of the first chapters of the story in 1893.

When she was young, her parents had a liking for the West Country, spending holidays at Falmouth, Torquay and Weymouth. But in 1882, having decided against East Anglia and also against Dawlish, they chose Ilfracombe and arrived there by train, on 3 April, to stay at a lodging house kept by a Mr. and Mrs. Hussell in Hillsborough Terrace, one of those 'handsome terraces' built half a century earlier, high above the harbour, with splendid views over the Bristol Channel.

Beatrix was not quite sixteen. She had already fully developed the gracefully written code language she used for her journal, which was to remain undeciphered until Leslie Linder found the key to it in 1958.[1] The fact that she took so much trouble to keep secret the wholly unsensational record of her opinions and the events of her quiet days indicates the intensity of her determination to preserve an inner life for herself apart from that of her parents.

The Potters visited West Down, Berrynarbor and Combe Martin; Beatrix made notes on the church in each place. Of Watermouth Castle she says, 'It was the residence of Mr. Basset, who had a large estate here. He was rather queer, they say he did not live at the Castle but at a little house further on. His horse ran away with him and broke his neck at the corner of a field'.[2]

The Hussells drew from her two thumbnail sketches that seem to foreshadow the Beatrix Potter of her creative years. She found it almost impossible not to laugh when talking to Mrs. Hussell, who spoke 'in the broadest Devonshire, though her remarks were mostly limited to "a-yesssm"'. A tiny old woman, she was 'humpbacked and energetic, slumping about at a great rate—very different is Mr. Hussell, a perfect model of a hotel waiter, obliging and talkative, with a sharp nose, a smiling face, carefully brushed hair, and always accompanied by a strong smell of hair oil'.

The following year Mrs. Potter and Beatrix arrived in Ilfracombe on 2 April, joined by Mr. Potter five days later. In the interval Beatrix wrote him a letter which included a description of the unloading of coal from a coaster on Watermouth beach. 'The tide was coming in very fast. One old lady who seemed very anxious to get her coal drove the horse and cart at full speed into the water making such a splashing'. Some years later she came across the letter and pencilled on the envelope 'Worth keeping, an early impression leading to Pig Robinson', and there is a sketch she made at this time with the note 'The harbour in Pig Robinson was a description of Ilfracombe' (though clearly the illustration used as a frontispiece to the book is not, and the line drawing of a collier aground, with a horse and cart beside it, which may be seen on page seven of *The Tale of Little Pig Robinson*, shows the scene described above, but the bay is much larger than Watermouth).

Little Pig Robinson was the last story she published, at a time when she was 'scraping together something to appease my publishers'. She dismissed it as 'most dreadful rubbish', yet it would be difficult to regard this early fantasy, which accounts for the presence of the pig that Lear's Owl and Pussycat discovered in the land where the Bong tree grows, as anything but delightful. It shows its author's imagination moving in a world where there is no distinction at all between animals and human beings: in Stymouth, animals are customers at shops kept by human beings, and vice versa. But the characteristic, astringent Beatrix Potter tone is to be found in it: for instance, Aunt Dorcas and Aunt Porcas, who own the farm, Piggery Porcombe, where Pig Robinson grows up, 'led prosperous uneventful lives, and their end was bacon'.

Like the rest of Britain, Ilfracombe celebrated Queen Victoria's Golden Jubilee in the summer of 1887 with the sort of festivities that had marked special occasions all through the century. As a more permanent memento of the day, it was decided to build a shelter to enable visitors 'to enjoy a promenade in inclement weather, besides providing a winter garden to assist in the restoration of the invalid to robust health'. Although the Great Exhibition of 1851 had demonstrated the possibilities of large glass and iron structures, W. H. Gould, architect and surveyor to Ilfracombe's Local Board, may have been influenced, in his planning of the Victoria Pavilion, more by the Palm House at Kew, designed by Decimus Burton and built in 1844–48, than by Paxton's Crystal Palace. However, whereas the Palm House is 360 feet long and 50 feet wide, the Promenade, set down under the lee of the Capstone, was of more modest proportions—200 feet by 30 feet. It provided a building of elegance and charm, where on wet days visitors—and, indeed, Ilfracombe residents—could stroll, or sit and talk, or read, or listen to music played by what was always known as the Season Band.

A question that exercised the local authority was whether to light the building with the now familiar gas, or to be adventurous and use electricity. Eventually, gas was decided on; the opening on a night in August 1888 provided 'a brilliant scene in the well-lighted Promenade', where 'a happy, well-dressed, well-behaved audience' listened to a concert, tickets for which had been sold in aid of the Tyrrell Cottage Hospital. Yet the *North Devon Journal* reporter shows a tendency to damn the place with faint praise. Ordinarily referred to simply as 'The Shelter', it soon acquired the nickname of 'the Cucumber Frame' (perhaps because Ruskin had referred to the Crystal Palace as 'a monstrous cucumber frame'). Like the bandstand erected at the same time, it was to be swept away in less than 80 years.

Apart from listening to music in the new Promenade and, in fine weather, at the bandstand, visitors and townspeople could go to concerts, and also plays and lectures, at several other places. The Assembly Rooms in Coronation Terrace possessed 'a well-appointed stage and scenery, with all the gas-fittings, etc., for the production of amateur or private theatricals'. In 1883 the Oxford Hall was built, seating 900, and after the completion of the large new *Runnacleave* hotel in the summer of 1891, the adjoining Runnacleave hall, which could seat between five and six hundred, was opened on Whit Monday 1892, with a concert given by professional singers.

Thousands of visitors had their first sight of Ilfracombe from the sea, as they sailed in aboard one of the big new paddle-steamers and disembarked at the new

ILFRACOMBE HOTEL.

INDIAN AND COLONIAL VISITORS desirous of seeing with comfort all the beauties of Coast and Inland Scenery which North Devon affords, will find that the natural centre to be chosen is **THE ILFRACOMBE HOTEL.** 250 Apartments. Handsome Public Rooms. Ornamental Grounds of 5 acres, extending to the Sea. Eight Lawn Tennis Courts. Large Swimming Bath. Private Baths. *Full descriptive Tariff of* MANAGER, **Ilfracombe, North Devon.**

28. This advertisement of 1895 shows that the *Ilfracombe Hotel* was by then hoping to attract visitors from distant lands of Victoria's empire.

pier. Quite apart from the frequent arrival of these ships all through the season, and of the packets that called regularly during the winter, the harbour still saw a good deal of activity, although it had ceased to be a registered port in 1839.[3] Its coasting trade went on, and its use as a refuge remained; when the weather was bad, according to W. J. Slade, a number of Appledore ketches might seek shelter and stay there quite happily for long periods.[4] The Bristol Channel pilot boats lay at anchor while waiting to put a pilot aboard a ship or take him off. And local fishermen sailed out to bring in catches, though probably these were by now mostly for local consumption. (Lilian Wilson, in her *Ilfracombe's Yesterdays,* recalls watching the unloading of herring boats in the harbour. She is speaking of her childhood, in Edwardian days, but even then the fish were so plentiful that they would be sold on the Quay at from 40 or even 60 a shilling, and there were still smoking and salting houses in use.)

But the shipyard, which had produced so many wooden sailing ships over the centuries, had fallen silent. The last commercial vessel to be built there was the *Cloffock,* a schooner of 101 tons launched in 1865; her builder was Thomas Cook of Appledore, who had taken over the yard from Charles Dennis in 1860. After that, John Pollard built a few small cutters for use in taking holiday-makers for trips. They were durable craft; according to Grahame Farr, two of them, the

Foam, built in 1878, and the *Polly,* built in 1893, were still afloat as yachts in 1976.[5]

From the early days of steamers, occasional excursions had been run from Bristol or South Wales to places on the north coast of Devon and to Lundy; in 1827, on the day the Duchess of Clarence passed through Barnstaple on her way to Ilfracombe, the *Lady Rodney* steam packet, owned by a firm in Newport, Monmouthshire, sailed up the Taw, and carried a party to Lundy the following day.[6] But as the number of people able to afford holidays increased, companies in Bristol, Cardiff and Swansea began to compete to offer them pleasure trips. In 1878 the Portishead Dock Company launched an iron paddler, *Lyn,* which had been built specially for the Ilfracombe run, though she had only a short life as an excursion steamer: after six years she was sold to become a ferry on the Bosphorus. In the 1880s a family named Campbell came south from the Clyde and set up business in Bristol. As the 1933 edition of their guide book put it, the development of their excursions in the Bristol Channel 'dates from the end of the 1887 season, when the *Waverley*, having successfully completed her charter for a number of local gentlemen, Messrs. P. and A. Campbell resolved to give the Bristol station a share of their personal attention. The *Waverley* had previously been engaged on the Clyde, where she was known as "the Clipper of the Clyde", and on coming to the West of England she earned the title of "the Greyhound of the Bristol Channel". Although competition waxed keen, the *Waverley* secured the almost unanimous support of the local marine excursionists'. She was so successful that Peter and Alec Campbell soon ordered the building of a new saloon steamer, the *Ravenswood,* which ran from Bristol on her first trip in July 1891.

Two years later the brothers turned their business into a limited company; by 1897 they were advertising that their summer season would begin with Easter trips from Ilfracombe to Wooda Bay, Lynmouth, Cardiff, Clevedon and Bristol, and that in the following week the 'powerful sea-going saloon steamer *Brighton,* would run to Swansea, Lundy, Lynmouth and Clovelly. The other 'palatial' paddlers making up their fleet, the announcement added, were the *Britannia, Cambria, Westward Ho!, Lady Margaret, Ravenswood* and *Waverley.* All these ships were to become familiar sights in Ilfracombe harbour over the next 17 years, after which they were to see service in the First World War.

The Campbells began to organise combined rail and steamer trips from Midland towns and cities: in July 1896, for instance, what was described as 'A Monster Excursion' left Birmingham at about 10.30 at night by special train to arrive at Bristol at 2 in the morning and board the *Cambria* and the *Britannia* (the latter had made her first call at Ilfracombe only the previous month). Each ship took about 800 excursionists. The sea was rough, and many passengers were seasick during the night crossing. However, when they arrived at Ilfracombe at six o'clock, they found breakfast provided for them in the Town Hall. They then had the whole day to indulge in whatever amusements they had energy for before embarking on their homeward voyage at 6 p.m.

For those who wanted less stamina-testing outings, the railways ran many excursion trains to and from the Midlands, the north of England and London, as well as to resorts on the south coast—Hastings, St Leonards, Brighton and Eastbourne. The South Western Railway offered cheap holiday tickets to the Channel Islands, via Southampton, leaving Ilfracombe on Saturdays and returning on any Saturday or Monday within the next 16 days.

And although rail travel had put an end to the stage coach, coaches were still both popular and useful for local trips of all kinds. In November 1875, Sam Colwill advertised that he had bought the business of 'Carriage and Jobmaster' from Mr. George Williams; the following summer he began his first season of excursions to Lynton. He had been for more than 20 years the driver of coaches running a regular service to Barnstaple. Now he began to drive his own coach, *Benita* (named after Benita Odam, Lorna Doone's nurse). This left the *Ilfracombe* hotel every morning except Sunday for Lynton, at 8.30 a.m. and returned at 6 p.m. His office, at which bookings could be made, was at 96 High Street.

Another firm, Lake and Copp, which by 1897 advertised itself as Copp's Coaching Trips, owned several coaches. Their *Defiance* left the coach office for Lynton daily at 9.45 a.m. and returned by 6.45 p.m.; the return fare was seven shillings, while a single journey was four and sixpence. Their *Katerfelto* ran daily to Watermouth. Their *Dreadnought*, built in 1891 by a local coach builder, J. Ellis, was smart in dark blue paint with red wheels and gold lettering; it was kept very busy, making trips to Woolacombe sands every Monday, Wednesday and Saturday; to Berry Down Cross and back via Combe Martin every Tuesday and Thursday; and to Barnstaple market on Fridays. 'The above Coaches will call at all hotels and boarding houses, and are the only Coaches that convey Great Western and South Western Railway Tourist Ticket passengers', the advertisements announced. And apart from Mr. Ellis, there was at least one other coach builder in the town: Eli Hill advertised his 'Ilfracombe Coach Factory' at 21 and 22 Church Street.

For those who preferred to be independent, there were private carriages for hire, as well as riding horses and, apparently, a variety of small vehicles drawn by animals other than horses. A contemporary guide book included by-laws regulating the number of passengers in any one carriage. The scale was as follows: one pony or mule or two asses, not more than three passengers; one ass, not more than one passenger; a goat or goats, not more than two children. (A note added that two children under the age of 10 might be regarded as one adult.) Contemplating the Ilfracombe hills, one feels sorry for the goats.

One entry gives rise to a momentary impression that Victorian Ilfracombe possessed a band of heroic Devonian rickshaw boys: it speaks of 'Hackney carriages drawn by asses *or by hand*', for which the fares were sixpence for any distance not exceeding half a mile; eightpence for more than half a mile but less than a mile; fourpence for each half-mile or part of a half-mile thereafter. Donkey carts had been part of the town's life since the Revd. Woolocombe described them in 1816, and probably long before that, and the vehicles propelled by human muscle were not pulled but pushed; some type of Bath chair in which the old or infirm might be pushed—very often by boys—around Capstone Parade,

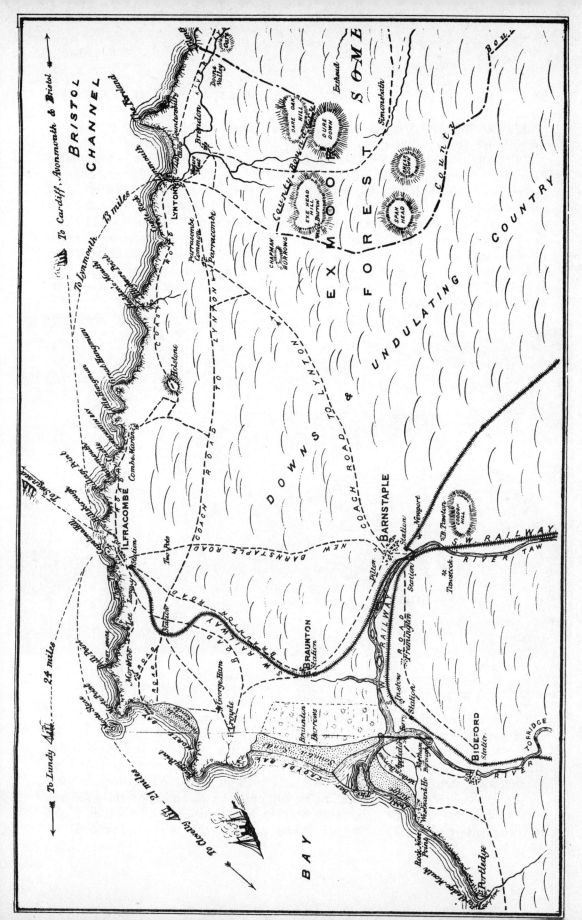

29. A map from a guide book of the late 19th century, showing sea, rail and coach routes to and from Ilfracombe.

or down to the pier, or along the High Street, or even up that long, long slope to the station high above the town.

All though the '90s Ilfracombe was growing rapidly. In 1889 the Wildercombe Park estate was sold as building land: 123 acres lying below the Cairn, alongside the road to Barnstaple, divided into 26 lots varying in size from a quarter of an acre to 27 acres. (The sale schedule estimated that 200,000 people visited the town every year. Less extravagantly, perhaps, a reporter in 1896 suggested that 'a floating population of upwards of 100,000 visitors annually pass through Ilfracombe, staying for shorter or longer periods'.) During the next 10 years building went on, not only at Wildercombe and St Brannocks adjoining, but also at Crofts Lea Park and Chambercombe Park to the east of the town. A few more houses were completed at Torrs Park.

30. The glass and iron winter garden, built in 1888 to celebrate Queen Victoria's Golden Jubilee. It had many names but it was usually known locally as the 'Shelter' or the 'Cucumber Frame'. Nothing now remains of it.

Hotel accommodation was also being increased; in 1891 the *Collingwood* hotel was enlarged, and the *Granville* and *Runnacleave* hotels opened. The *Granville* was announced as a much-needed temperance hotel; it was named after Dr. Granville, a leading figure in the 19th-century temperance movement. The *Runnacleave*, designed by W. H. Gould, and built on what had been Runnacleave Meadow, was described as a boarding house, not a hotel, and apparently did not seek to compete with the *Ilfracombe* hotel in luxuriousness; nevertheless, it had its own pleasure yacht, *Wanderer*, which was 'placed at the disposal of visitors'.

Under the provisions of the Local Government Act of 1894, the old local Board of Health, established in 1851, became the Ilfracombe Urban District Council, with 15 members. It adopted as the town arms a device consisting of a quartered shield: the first quarter black, a silver fess between three silver battle axes erect, with red hafts, for the family of Wrey; the second silver with six single-masted ships, representing the ships which Ilfracombe provided for Edward III's French wars; the third silver, a red engrailed cross between four black water budgets, for the family of Bourchier; and the fourth silver, three blue wavy bars and an oar lying in bend sinister, for the seal of the old Local Board of Health. The shield is flanked by two dolphins, head downwards, and beneath is the motto *'Ilfracombe potens salubritate'*—Ilfracombe strong for health.[7] (The Bourchier arms had dolphins as supporters.)

At this time there was a possibility that private speculators might use the green slopes of Hillsborough as housing sites. One of the new Council's first acts was to buy the headland for £7,500. They also leased the west side of the Cairn from a local solicitor, E. W. Veale, and began to lay it out as a pleasure ground, cutting paths, planting trees and setting up public seats. (Later they were to become the owners of the whole of the Cairn.)

A Town Advertising Committee was formed in 1896, and published 25,000 copies of a pamphlet setting out the attractions of Ilfracombe. That summer it was reported that the paddle-steamers were bringing more day trippers than ever—yet there were fewer staying visitors. 'The amount of business done at the *Ilfracombe* hotel is a very good guide to the season's trade, and the company has had to report such a falling-off in its receipts as to reduce its annual dividend to four per cent.'. (Only a few years earlier it had been seven per cent.)

In fact, looking back at the end of 1896, one reporter designated it 'a record year for bad trade and misfortune'. The worst misfortune had been headlined in the *North Devon Journal* as 'The Great Fire at Ilfracombe'. It had started in the furniture and ironmongery shop of Mr. Coles, at the corner of Portland Street, at about one o'clock in the morning. The fire brigade had been summoned, only to find no water available: the previous Saturday the District Council had decreed that the mains should be turned off for five hours each night to avoid waste. There was no telephone to Slade Reservoir, and it was an hour before a message was acted on (one can only assume that the messenger walked: on horseback, or even on a bicycle, he could have been there in half the time). By the time the brigade had a chance to use their hoses, the fire had a powerful hold; it had leaped across the High Street and was blazing down the Arcade and through properties on either side. More than 30 shops and houses were gutted; the ruins went on smouldering for several days, and unsafe buildings had to be pulled down. Yet it seems remarkable, in view of the limited effectiveness of the small, horse-drawn fire engines of the time, that the conflagration was checked as soon as it was, and that there were neither deaths nor serious injury. (In the fire of September 1983, that so strangely began in almost the same place—the site of origin being the Arcade itself with flames running north to destroy the *Candar* hotel—20 pumping appliances, two turntable ladders and seven ambulances were rushed to Ilfracombe; one young man died while trying to ensure that there was no one still asleep in a blazing building, and a number of firemen were injured.) However, the sheer size of the fire, and the loss of property and trade, dismayed the townspeople, despite the fact that a relief fund was at once set up and many holiday-makers staying at the various hotels subscribed generously.[8]

The following year, with rebuilding going on and the Queen's Diamond Jubilee to be celebrated, life was happier. In the summer of 1897 the whole of Britain was drawn into an exultant outburst of merrymaking. In Ilfracombe it was the last great jollification of the century, outdoing in splendour even such occasions as the opening of the pier and the railway. Apart from bonfires, fireworks, balls, processions, teas and other festivities, the town was decorated from end to end; every lamp-post was wound round with evergreens and flowers, banners were flown from innumerable buildings, and 2,000 'variegated gas lamps' were hung in front of the Victoria Pavilion and the Town Hall. Finally, no fewer than 20 arches were set up at intervals along the streets; they stretched from the railway station to the *Britannia,* and each had its motto: 'Victoria the Good, Upon whose empire the sun never sets, Revered of all Nations, Loved and Honoured . . .' on and on it stretched, from the Cairn to the harbour, one enormous sentence of loyal fervour.

Chapter Twelve

INTO THE TWENTIETH CENTURY

ILFRACOMBE BEGAN the 20th century with an extensive and, for the size of the town, expensive programme of public works. By May 1901, a large new market house, begun in the previous year, had been completed. Lying on the hill between Market Street and Avenue Road, it was built on more than one level to compensate for the steepness of the slope. It was named the Alexandra Hall in honour of Edward VII's queen: the nation had mourned the death of Queen Victoria the previous January. The new hall did not merely accommodate the market; the lower part of the building, with a wood-blocked floor, contained a stage and could provide seating for some 1,400 people, giving the town yet another place of entertainment. It was soon in frequent use, with concerts by visiting celebrities; Kreisler played there in October 1904.

To supply its increasing population and enhance its image as an outstandingly healthy and health-giving resort (*Ilfracombe potens salubritate*) the Council carried out a scheme of drainage and waterworks considerably more ambitious than those undertaken in the previous century, and to emphasise its go-ahead character, it also arranged for the introduction of electric light.

As far as the latter was concerned, things went rapidly and smoothly. The Council came to an agreement with the Edmundson Electric Corporation and allotted them a site in Hospital Road. Within a year the works were completed and in operation; by June 1903 the *Ilfracombe* hotel was having electricity installed, and it was reported that the grounds at the front were 'brilliantly illuminated at night by two powerful lamps on tall columns'. Although the town's streets continued for many years to be lit by gas, as did a high proportion of houses, the gasworks was moved to a new site at Hele, the old one off Church Street being bought by the Council for £2,500.

New sources of water for Ilfracombe had been sought for some time when in August 1900 the Ilfracombe Improvement Act authorised the town to take the headwaters of the Bray by eight intakes embracing a watershed of some 3,000 acres near Challacombe. It proved necessary to cut a tunnel 590 yards long near Friendship Farm; a Cornish firm from Camborne was given the contract, and, with the precision of those days, the cost of this was reported as £4,729 2s. 11d. The engineers had to lay a pipe-line 14 miles in length; taking in the parishes of Combe Martin and Berrynarbor, it ran to Mullacott Cross and so to the two reservoirs at Slade, the total capacity of which was by now over 54 million gallons. The whole project cost about £55,000, and was finished by the summer of 1904.

So satisfied was the Council with the considerable engineering feat it had called into being that it hoped for the good fortune of a royal opening: Edward VII had, after all, visited Ilfracombe, albeit very briefly, in his boyhood. However, the king had an engagement in Wales on the appointed day, and so the Lord Lieutenant of Devon, Lord Ebrington, was invited to perform the ceremony. Lord Clifford, Edward Soares, the M.P. for North Devon, and the Devon-born General Sir Redvers Buller, as well as a large number of local notables, were present—but what was perhaps more important from the Council's point of view was the fact that the Medical Officers of Health of London, Birmingham and Nottingham accepted invitations to attend.

As it happened, the day chosen for the opening, 27 July 1904, was very wet, but the eminent visitors and the large crowd of onlookers did not seem to mind; speeches included jokes about an abundant water supply. A platform had been erected at the western end of the Promenade, immediately above Wildersmouth beach, and on the beach a small fountain had been built; when Lord Ebrington inaugurated the water works by pressing a button to operate this fountain, the jet spurted generously and, caught by the wind, made everyone even wetter than they had been, but it was all taken in good part.

Within the following year the new drainage scheme was completed, at a cost of £30,000, and by 1907 Ilfracombe was advertising itself as a resort noted for its warm winter climate, its delightful scenery and the purity, not only of its air, but also of its water and 'modern scientific sanitation'. This advertisement, which included a long list of the town's amenities—Winter Gardens, Promenade Bands, Concerts, 'High-class Theatrical Performances and other Select Entertainments', bathing, boating, bowls, cricket, fishing, tennis, and golf (this last was played on a course on the Combe Martin side of Hillsborough)[1]—appeared in a stout volume entitled *A Book of the South West,* printed for the 75th annual meeting of the British Medical Association, which was held at Exeter in 1907. It contained essays on the history, scenery and climatology of Devon and Cornwall, with a section on 'The influence of climates on health and disease'. In the notes on Ilfracombe it is observed that 'Two points in the statistics are of special medical interest, *viz.* the remarkable frequency of old age, and the low death-rates from tubercular diseases. During the years 1901 to 1904, out of 463 deaths, 40 per cent. were at ages over 65, nine per cent. over 80, and three per cent. between 90 and 100; in the churchyard there are records of six lives over 100'. This was, in fact, an understatement: no fewer than nine centenarians since 1784 had already been recorded, and in 1913 the total was to be brought to ten. Two slate tablets clamped to the outside of the east wall of the parish church still record their names.[2]

The Council saw a possibility of promoting interest in Ilfracombe's salubrious qualities, and invited a number of medical men who had attended the Exeter conference to spend a day in the town. They were entertained to lunch at the *Ilfracombe* hotel, and, after an afternoon of sightseeing, to tea at the *Cliffe Hydro.* Opened in 1905, this was a hotel with a difference, designed to attract as guests at all seasons of the year those who were in search of the hydropathic treatment then much favoured for a variety of complaints. No doubt the owner, Dr. Toller, took pride in showing his visiting colleagues the *Hydro's* 'complete installation of electric baths and all modern appliances for the treatment of neuritis, gout, etc.'.

In the same year of 1907, the Board of Trade gave Ilfracombe Council permission to make an important purchase from the Weld family (the descendants of Sir Bourchier Palk Wrey)—the pier and the harbour. The town had been leasing the property for two years at a rent of £1,750 a year, with an option to buy. At a Board of Trade enquiry, the chairman of the Council, J. C. Clarke, gave evidence that sea traffic was developing fast, much of it coming from towns around the Bristol Channel, with what he referred to as half-day trips arriving from Birmingham by rail and steamer. He quoted the figures of passengers landing at the promenade pier: 94,000 in 1902; 93,000 in 1903; 112,508 in 1904; 140,877 in 1905; and 164,745 in 1906, figures that emphasise the immense and rapidly-increasing popularity of the big, comfortable paddle-steamers of Edwardian days.

The pier was regarded as a particularly valuable acquisition, since a small admission fee had always been charged. It was reported to be in good condition, supported as it was by piles attached to a natural reef of rock. The investment made in the early 1870s now appeared to be a timely one, increasing the town's holiday trade in the way its supporters had envisaged.

31. The arms of Ilfracombe adopted in 1894 when, under the Local Government Act, the local Board of Health (established in 1851) became the Ilfracombe District Council.

During the summer months, and especially after Bank Holidays, the local newspaper gave the names of the various excursion steamers, sailing from Bristol, Cardiff and Newport, that had called at Ilfracombe. The *North Devon Journal*, for instance, reported in August 1905 that over the Bank Holiday the *Normandy, Brighton, Ravenswood, Gwalia, Albion, Westward Ho!* and *Britannia* had all visited the harbour, each carrying anything from 400 to 800 passengers. Some of the latter had stayed aboard to cruise along the coast of north Devon, other trippers from Ilfracombe joining them. Meanwhile a great number had chosen to go sightseeing on land. The proprietors of horse-drawn coaches had run trips to Watersmouth, Combe Martin, the Sterridge Valley, Lynton, Hunter's Inn, Lee and Woolacombe, and had been so busy that they had been compelled to turn away many prospective passengers.

A few weeks earlier, however, a letter had appeared in the paper calling attention to the problem that had troubled some people for a number of years, especially since the Welsh Sunday Closing Act of 1881. It was a great pity, the writer said, 'that something cannot be done to prevent the "dumping" at Ilfracombe of a very undesirable class of day tripper—the one who lands here much the worse for liquor. Unfortunately the licensing laws do not run at sea, and trippers can apparently get as much as they like on board. It may be, of course, that they carry it with them, but such trippers as those who made Broad Street and the Quay a pandemonium for drunken behaviour, fighting and bad language on a recent day need to be dealt with severely, if the quiet of the town is to be maintained'.

But although the complaint was sometimes made that the steamers sailing in from Wales, especially on Sundays, were nothing but floating beer shops (in 1896 a question had even been asked in the House of Commons about it) the majority of passengers presumably behaved decently enough to prevent the trippers from becoming too unpopular.

For several years, to the end of Edward VII's reign, the numbers of people passing through the turnstiles of Ilfracombe's pier continued to rise, summer by summer, and the town was steadily prosperous, despite the necessity, in 1910, to borrow money to repair the havoc caused by a freak storm that battered many coastal places. One December evening, when an exceptionally high tide was being driven onshore by a furious westerly to north-westerly gale, a sudden great surge swept in across Wildersmouth and flooded Capstone Parade, Ropery Meadow and the baths and esplanade of the *Ilfracombe* hotel, ripping up roadways and demolishing masonry. The sea wall at Cheyne Beach was broken in several places and the pier was damaged.

April 1911 saw the opening of Ilfracombe's first cinema: 'a Picture Hall was opened in Northfield Road, and it has provided high-class entertainment of the popular kind', a local newspaper observed. Moreover, during that summer 'ample provision was made for the entertainment of visitors by concerts at the Pavilion, the Gaiety Hall, the Runnacleave Hall, the Alexandra Hall, on Montebello Lawn and on the Pier'.

The concerts given by the Season Band in the Pavilion and at what was known as the North Bandstand, to distinguish it from the bandstand on the pier, were evidently immensely popular in the years before the First World War. They often included four songs written in Edwardian days by an author-composer called H. Verne: 'Watersmeet', 'The Witches of Lyn', 'Dear Old Ilfracombe' (described as 'a quaint ditty in the old English style') and 'Clovelly'. According to the publishers, the latter had been several times noticed in the Bristol press as likely to do for north Devon what Balfe's 'Killarney' had done for the west of Ireland; many thousands of copies had been sent to all parts of the world, and 'the enormous increase in the number of visitors to the famous spot' was undoubtedly largely due to the popularity of this song. Visitors were advised to hear it 'sung to orchestral accompaniment, if possible at the North Bandstand, where the scene is sometimes most remarkable'.

Verne's songs were originally published individually by J. T. White at what he called his 'Music Warerooms' at Ilfracombe, Barnstaple and Bideford, but they were later distributed by a London firm, Warren and Phillips. They were successful enough to be republished as a collection, *Verne's Souvenir Songs of Devon*, sold as 'a novel and artistic form of souvenir that no other pleasure resort offers'; this bears no date, but as it includes 'Hail to the King', written to celebrate George V's coronation, it probably appeared at some time between 1910 and 1914.

Another composer, Allen T. Hussell, set to music words by Will H. Coates, the writer of the dialect account in rhyme of Alfred Price's fight on Rapparee with the future Kaiser. Songs by Hussell and Coates include 'The Vale of Fuchsias (Dear little Lee)' and 'Coachman Sam', written after the death, in 1919, of Sam Colwill (*see* Appendix). It seems that in 1911, at the age of 85, Sam Colwill had at last decided to retire from his coachman's box: for the first time for 57 years, a reporter noted, no splendid four-in-hand coaches, drawn by Sam's famous grey horses, made day trips to Lynton; smaller vehicles replaced them. And by that time motor traffic was increasing; excursions were being run 'as far afield as to Dartmoor for the day'.

32. Apart from the fact that the wall is no longer battlemented, the way down to the Tunnels beach has not changed much since this drawing was made in 1860, and reproduced by Gadsby.

The 1912 season was wet, with a consequent fall in the number of visitors, but 1913 was outstandingly successful: 'As if in defiance of all those who say that the number 13 in unlucky, Ilfracombe is able to look back over a season that has been a record one as regards numbers. One of the distinctive signs of the times is the increase in what may be called "Co-operative" holidays, and of such parties Ilfracombe has had a good and growing share, chiefly from the great towns of Lancashire'.

The early motor coaches, always known as charabancs, had been busy; pier takings were more than £600 above those of 1912, and the *Ilfracombe* hotel announced a considerable increase in trade. The success of the *Northfield* picture house had encouraged the opening of a rival, the *Palace* cinema, in a building previously known as the 'Posada'. The only slight cause of dissatisfaction was that the rail services were considered inadequate; the Council made representations to both the London and South Western and the Great Western, asking for more frequent and faster trains. In 1914, until the month of July, the town enjoyed another good holiday season. Suddenly, at the end of the month, the paddle-steamers stopped calling. Within a week, for Ilfracombe, as for the whole of Britain, life abruptly changed.

The outbreak of war with Germany on 4 August—the Great War, as newspapers at once began to call it—necessarily had an immediate effect on the holiday trade of all seaside resorts, and especially on that minority, like Ilfracombe, that relied heavily on sea-borne visitors. But the tone of the summary of the year's events, written by a journalist who was, as usual, anonymous, makes the war sound like a personal affront to Ilfracombe:

> The year will long be remembered as the most disastrous on record, from a business point of view, although the earlier part of the season gave promise of being the best ever known. Down to the end of July everything was flourishing and season bookings were good, but as soon as War broke out rooms were cancelled wholesale and only in very rare cases was any compensation paid, even of the smallest kind. A very few of the intending visitors came on later, but the total loss to the town must have been many thousands of pounds.

At the end of the following year, after an almost identical opening, the writer went on to say that in some respects things had been much worse than in 1914, 'for in that year the service of boats was maintained to the end of July. But no steamers at all came during the past summer, and the many traders who specially cater for boat passengers have felt the loss very severely. The general ratepayers will suffer when the end of the financial year in March next shows the heavy loss to the pier funds from the same cause. The lack of excursion fares (i.e., on trains) made a great difference to the number of visitors arriving, although this was not so noticeable during the very few weeks called "the height of the season". It had been hoped that the comparative insecurity of some other health resorts would have been to the benefit of Ilfracombe, but this hope was not realised'. (1915, it may be recalled, was the year of the battles of Neuve Chapelle, Loos and Second Ypres, and the disaster of Gallipoli.)

The summary for 1916 deplored the fact that the town had 'suffered severely' for the past three seasons 'although not within what may be called a "danger area" of the War'. The charabancs could no longer run: petrol supplies had been stopped. But at last, in this year when hundreds of thousands of men had spent 'the height of the season' fighting and dying on the Somme, it was acknowledged that there were other forms of suffering than reduction of trade: 'Many homes in the town have had to mourn the loss of a loved one—husband, son or brother— by the war, and the sorrow has only been lightened by the knowledge that each man gave his life in the best of all sacrifices, for the welfare of the country he loved'. One can only suppose that the writer of these annual reports was an elderly man with no one dear to him serving in any theatre of war.

33.   It was not until Edwardian times that this beach ceased to be the ladies' bathing beach, or cove—another beach further west being allotted to men—and became known simply as the Tunnels, open to everyone.

According to Lilian Wilson, Ilfracombe was very lucky in both wars, experiencing fewer food shortages, in particular, than many other places. During the First World War, when she worked in a munitions factory in London, she was sent welcome food parcels from home which she shared with others in the house where she was staying. She mentions an interesting aspect of the time: the receipt, by one of the newspaper shops—Bryants at No. 85, the High Street—of telegrams announcing the latest news, good or bad; these, posted up in the shop window, gave information of events 24 hours before they appeared in the newspapers themselves, and drew crowds eager to read them.

The ordinary people of Ilfracombe did the sort of things that were being done all over Britain to help the war effort: they collected funds to send extra food and clothing to soldiers on active service, they knitted socks and gloves and made shirts, they bought War Bonds, and they put up with such shortages and food rationing as were unavoidable. At Craigmore, St Brannocks, a V.A.D. hospital was opened, with 24 beds.

As for the young men who went out of the town early in the war as volunteers, their letters, published in the local newspapers, show them accepting the dangers and hardships of their new life in a way that makes them sound like members of a different order of being from the writer of the year-end summaries. Here, for instance, is Driver Sollis, a former pupil of Holy Trinity Boys' School, writing to his old headmaster:

> We have had a week's rest and a good clean up, which we were very glad to get, I can tell you. We go back to the fighting tomorrow, to give the Germans a good Xmas box. Our battery, the 114th, has done some good work and we hope to do more. Tucker and I are in the same gun team, so we are lucky. When we get home again, I expect we shall take some time getting out of bed. We have had some very cold weather here—snow four or five inches deep, and the roads covered with ice, so that the horses could not stand. But it is getting better now that all the snow is gone away. It is not very nice when you get up in the morning and find that your boots are frozen so that you cannot get them on, and when you pick up your overcoat you can stand it upright, so you can tell it is a bit 'parky' out here. But we are happy as larks, and getting used to the 'Jack Johnsons' [German shells]. It is awful to see the poor people that have been turned out of their homes. The people of England must think themselves lucky that it is not home (for them) there.

He goes on to say, hopefully, that he does not think the war can last much longer, only to negate that hope by adding that the Germans 'must be able to buy their soldiers ready-made, because as soon as one regiment is cut down another comes up in its place: you don't know where they come from'.

It is an interesting contrast in attitudes to be found in the pages of one provincial newspaper: while their elders at home lament their reduced takings, Driver Sollis and his fellows, in their frozen foreign trenches, are happy as larks. Fortunately, it seems that Driver Sollis survived the war; at least his name is not among the 157 on the town's memorial to its First World War dead.

Chapter Thirteen

BETWEEN THE WARS

AT THE BEGINNING of the First World War, the White Funnel Fleet of P. and A. Campbell numbered 13 paddle-steamers. Six had been requisitioned by the end of 1914, and were fitted out as mine-sweepers; five more were taken into service in 1915, and the remaining two, the *Waverley* and the *Glen Rosa,* began minesweeping and patrolling duties westward of Ilfracombe in 1917, later moving to the mouth of the Thames. The *Devonia,* which had made her first trip to Ilfracombe as a newly-launched vessel in May 1905, gave her name to a unit which included her sister ships *Westward Ho!, Brighton Queen, Cambria* and *Glen Avon.* Only two of the whole fleet were lost: the *Brighton Queen* was blown up in October 1915, while sweeping off Ostend, and not long afterwards the *Lady Ismay* similarly hit a mine and blew up; in both cases the crew were rescued. All but one of the surviving paddlers continued in service around the British coasts for the remainder of the war.

The exception, the *Barry,* had a particularly eventful career. Her first task was to transport German prisoners to Dublin, but in July 1915 she was sent to the Dardanelles, where she was engaged in running ammunition and stores, often under heavy fire, to Suvla Bay and Anzac beach. Out of commission for a while as the result of a collision, she was repaired and went back in time to help in the evacuation of British troops after the disastrous ending of the Dardanelles expedition; she was the last ship to leave Suvla Beach, taking the beachmaster and the rearguard with her. She served in the eastern Mediterranean until, in September 1919, she was returned to her owners to be renovated and repainted, like most of the remaining White Funnel Fleet, for the old peaceful business of carrying holiday-makers. She was re-named the *Waverley,* as the older ship of that name had ended her war service—as had the *Glen Rosa* and the *Albion*—in such a battered condition that she could no longer be used to carry passengers.[1]

In the summer of 1919, Ilfracombe was delighted to find that visitors were flooding in as never before. The *Ilfracombe* hotel nearly doubled its receipts for the year, but owing to the higher cost of supplies, wages and so on, the directors cautiously declared a dividend of only five per cent., 'putting a good sum to reserve'. During the previous five years, the town's ownership of the pier had not been a paying proposition; in 1918 there was a deficit of £2,000. But at a meeting of the Harbour Committee in July, a councillor exclaimed jubilantly, 'The Campbells are coming!' and soon not only the White Funnel Fleet of the Campbells, but the Yellow Funnel Fleet of W. H. Tucker and Co.

105

of Cardiff were bringing in day trippers in their thousands each week. Almost two-thirds of the deficit was wiped out that summer, and in 1920, when excursion steamers began to run at Easter for the first time since 1914, a profit of £700 was made.

Within a few years Campbells had overcome their rivals and bought from them two ships, the *Lady Moyra* and the *Lady Evelyn,* which they re-named the *Brighton Queen* and the *Brighton Belle* (Brighton was the headquarters of their other excursion steamer enterprise, which served a number of South Coast resorts). They also ordered a new paddle-steamer, the *Glen Gower,* which made her maiden voyage from Bristol to Ilfracombe in June 1922. According to Grahame Farr, she was to make a crossing from Ilfracombe to the Mumbles in August 1926, of one hour 17 minutes, a record never beaten by any paddle-steamer.[2]

Yet even in the 1920s, if steam made the outer harbour a place of bustling activity in the months of summer, sail kept alive all through the year the tradition of centuries of trade. A report of a dinner given to local seamen by the vicar of St Philip and St James in January 1928, includes the names of some two dozen vessels of various kinds, with their masters and crew members. No fewer than six of these mariners are named Williams—George, of the *Diana*; Bob, of the *Irene*; Tom, of the *Pear*; Leslie, of the *Ilfra*; William, of the *Florence*; and Sydney, of the *Grace Darling*—while four bear the familiar Ilfracombe name of Barbeary— J. L. Barbeary of the pleasure yacht *Foam*, built in Ilfracombe; Charles of the *Ellen*; T. H. W. Barbeary of the *Minnie*; and N. Barbeary of the *Saucy Lass.* The long-lived *Snowflake,* built of steel on the Clyde in 1893—a genuine Clyde 'puffer', in fact—which is well remembered even today by some of the older generation, is among the vessels named, with her master, James Irwin, who for some reason was nicknamed Tulip, and two of her crew, W. Pennington and D. Hooper.[3]

(By 1934 she was in the managing ownership of John Irwin of Combe Martin. Her cargo was usually coal, but in the '30s, at least, she underwent a remarkable transformation each summer. Her blackened hold washed clean and painted white, she carried thousands of baskets of strawberries, grown on the warm slopes above Combe Martin, to markets in South Wales—and, no doubt, brought some to Ilfracombe for sale there and in Barnstaple.)

In Ilfracombe, as elsewhere, there was concern during the early 1920s over unemployment, especially among those returning from the war. An Unemployment Grants Committee had been set up, to which applications could be made for help with public works. When the Council planned the laying out of the Victoria Pleasure Grounds on Ropery Meadow, with bowling and putting greens, this Committee gave a grant towards the cost on condition that preference was given to local unemployed ex-servicemen. Work began in January 1922, and was completed within a few months.

Two years later a garden of a different kind offered work for a while; rather later than some of its neighbours, Ilfracombe set up a war memorial. The collection of public subscriptions had begun in 1919, but for various reasons the project had been delayed. Originally, according to the *North Devon Herald,* it was intended to place the memorial on the sea front, but this idea met with a great deal of opposition on the ground that the centre of the summer season's pleasure ground was not a suitable site. The Council therefore acquired from the Ecclesiastical Commissioners some land on the slope to the south of the parish church, and there a granite column surmounted by a bronze winged figure of Victory was unveiled by Lord Fortescue on Armistice Day, 1924—a characteristically wet, drear November day. Bronze panels bearing the names of the 157 men from Ilfracombe parish who had died on active service during the war were affixed later. Around the memorial a Garden of Remembrance was laid out. (After the Second World War it was necessary to add three small panels to the base of the plinth supporting the granite column. They bore the names of 59 men and one woman—a member of the A.T.S.—who died on active service between 1939 and 1945.)

Although lack of jobs caused some hardship, by today's standards the number of unemployed was small. In 1924, the town had 130 out of work (112 men, 2 boys, 16 women, and no girls); the following year the total was 122 (91 men, 1 boy, 28 women, and 2 girls).

In general the people of Ilfracombe were apparently living fairly comfortably. In the summer months, visitors were continuing to pour in by train and steamer— and now, increasingly, by car. Commercial confidence was reflected in the founding of a local branch of the Chamber of Trade, which held its first annual dinner in April 1925.

The following month a 'palatial new concert hall', as the *North Devon Journal* described it, was opened. Designed by a London firm of architects, it cost over £8,000 to build, and seated 750. It was said to have been designed to harmonise with 'the balustrading that surrounded the bowling and putting greens of the recently completed Pleasure Grounds'. It certainly did not harmonise with the structure less than 40 years old, which it partially replaced, and which had been known by so many names—the Victoria Promenade, the Victoria Pavilion, the Winter Gardens, the Shelter, and the Cucumber Frame. Ornamented by two meaningless turrets, it sat between the glass wings which were allowed to survive for a few decades longer, presenting what Pevsner was later to call 'a chaste and somewhat joyless facade' towards the town.

Although the *Ilfracombe* hotel still tried to live up to the telegraphic address it had borne since it was first opened, 'Bestotel', it was now 50 years old, and its High Victorian standards of luxury were beginning to seem dated; if no other hotel in the town could equal it in actual number of rooms, several were almost as large and could offer comparable comfort and more modern interiors. Nevertheless, in the late 1920s, there was a move on the part of the local authority to buy it. At a meeting on 7 February 1928 a Special Committee's recommendation was laid before the Council to offer the Ilfracombe Hotel Company the sum of £43,500 for the whole of their interests, including furniture and fittings. Various suggestions were made for its use: the Council might simply run it as a hotel, or let part of it as a boarding establishment and part as a dance and concert room, or they might turn it into council offices. When their offer was turned down, the Council decided instead to lease the westernmost part of the hotel building, the tennis courts, the swimming baths and part of the promenade on the north side for £1,250 a year, with an option to purchase. They converted their section of the main building into municipal offices, moving in in May 1931.

Surprisingly, Ilfracombe as yet possessed neither a public library nor a museum. In 1904 an offer of £3,000 had been made by the Carnegie Trust for a library building. Unaccountably, because this did not include the money for a site, it was turned down; the Council declared at the time that it would 'adopt the Free Libraries Act'. Yet a quarter of a century had passed, and nothing had apparently been done.

A newcomer who settled in the town in 1930 decided that it was time to remedy this omission. Mervyn Grove Palmer was a naturalist who had acted as agent for the British Museum of Natural History, making journeys to many countries of South America to collect specimens. He first made it his business to arouse interest in the creation of a museum, and by February 1931 a working committee had been set up to get the project going. One difficulty was to find a suitable building: various places were suggested, including even the ancient chapel of St Nicholas, but in May 1932 the Council agreed that part of the disused laundry of the *Ilfracombe* hotel should be used. The collection and arrangement of exhibits went ahead during the rest of the year. There was an experimental day of opening on 1 August 1932, with free admission, which brought in no fewer than 1,231 visitors, but a formal opening ceremony was performed on 19 April 1933 in the concert room of the *Ilfracombe* hotel, by North Devon's M.P., Sir Basil Peto. Naturally enough, Mervyn Palmer was appointed the first curator. There was still no charge for admission, and the museum was much visited. Its collection of exhibits grew so rapidly that within two years the museum committee was complaining that it was already short of space. Within two years a small branch of the Devon County Library was established in the wing of the *Ilfracombe* hotel that housed the Council offices, and Mervyn Palmer proceeded to combine the duties of librarian with those of museum curator.

During the inter-war years Ilfracombe, like most of Britain, experienced the effects of a rapid increase in motor transport. It had seen its first motor buses as early as 1903. From the time of the opening of the narrow gauge Lynton to Barnstaple Railway in 1898, passengers had travelled by horse-drawn coach to Blackmoor Gate station. Sir George Newnes decided to set up a company to run motor buses instead. The service operated two open Milnes-Daimlers of 16 horse power. When local magistrates inflicted a heavy fine because one of these buses was said to have exceeded the speed limit (then eight miles an hour) Sir George disgustedly sold the buses to the motor department of the Great Western Railway.

Drawn by handsome grey horses, Sam Colwill's excursion coaches had been a familiar sight in and around Ilfracombe since the late 1870s. But he also began to run horse buses to villages in the area at the end of Victoria's reign. In the early years of the 20th century he replaced these with motor vehicles; by this time he had an office at 107 High Street and a garage in Marlborough Road. A year after his death in 1919, at the age of 93, a company was formed to buy the business from his widow for the sum of £3,600. Four years later it was sold for almost four times that amount. The new owners were the Hardy Central Garage of Minehead, who chose Barnstaple as their head office and adopted the name Hardy-Colwill.

In July 1927 the business changed hands yet again to what was then the National Omnibus and Transport Company; on 1 January 1929 this undertaking set up the Southern National Bus Company, among others, which soon extended the service of buses throughout north Devon, running Leyland Titan double deckers on the regular route from Ilfracombe to Westward Ho!, via Braunton, Barnstaple and Bideford on which buses still run today.[4]

Immediately after the First World War horse-drawn and motorised coaches competed with one another for a time, according to a guide book of about 1919, which observed 'Notwithstanding the advent of the motor charabanc, coaching retains much of its old popularity in Ilfracombe', and listed 11 places to which the 'numerous conveyances' ran. The charabancs carried from 20 to 30 passengers, and made trips as far as Bude; there was also a circular tour of Exmoor via Simonsbath, returning through South Molton.

Motor transport was, in fact, the greatest factor for change in the pattern of holiday-making. Admittedly a very large number of visitors still came by train—Ilfracombe was served by both the Southern and the Great Western Railways, and in 1926 the former began to run the Atlantic Coast Express, which carried passengers from Waterloo to Ilfracombe in seven hours. From South Wales and the Midlands the paddle-steamers continued to bring those who preferred a comparatively short sea crossing to the longer rail journey. However, there was an increasing number of people who, having arrived in their own cars, could use them to tour the surrounding countryside. The larger hotels began to inform prospective guests that they were 'officially appointed by the R.A.C. and A.A.' and possessed either their own lock-up garages (one was able to boast 'Own garage adjoining accommodating 70 cars with full repair and servicing facilities'), or parking space, or at the very least that there was a garage close by.

In guide books of the period advertisements appear for some 20 medium to large hotels, with anything from 40 to 200 rooms. There were about the same number of smaller establishments, calling themselves private hotels or guest houses, and nearly 200 offering board residence, furnished apartments or simply bed and breakfast. Prices lay within what today seems a narrow range, a reminder of the fact that one shilling, today's five pence, was then worth considerably more than the one pound coin of the late 20th century. Bed and breakfast, for instance, could be had for as little as 3s. or 3s. 6d., and was not likely to cost more than 5s. A 'quiet homely boarding house, taking only 10 guests' announced that its terms for a week's full board were 42s. to 60s., according to room and season. A small hotel might charge two and a half to three and a half guineas, while even the *Ilfracombe* hotel quoted its inclusive terms as beginning at four and a half guineas a week.

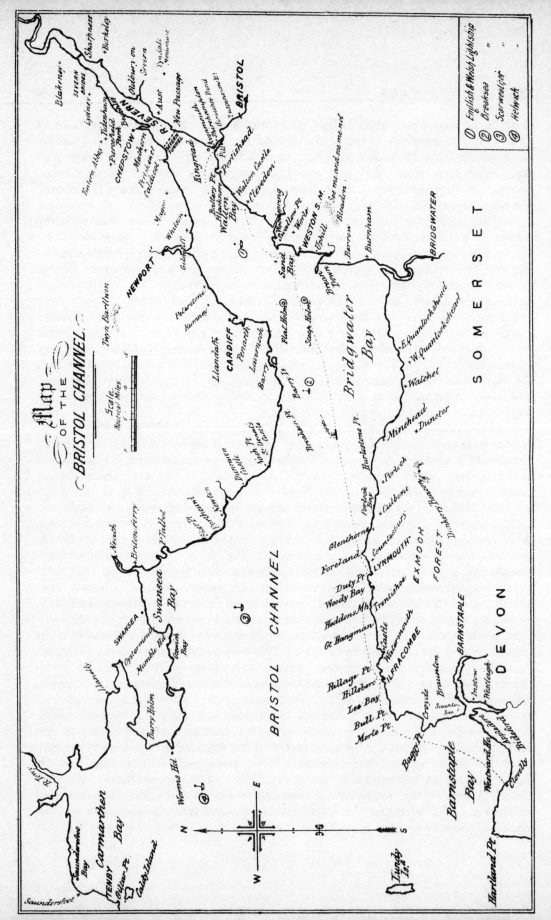

34. A map of the Bristol Channel from a late 19th-century guide to Ilfracombe, when paddle steamers linked the town with a dozen ports, large and small, along both shores of the Channel.

When in September 1939 Britain found itself at war with Germany for the second time in 25 years, it soon became clear that Ilfracombe's way of life would be more directly affected than it had been in 1914–18, when most hotels had been able to stay open and holiday-making, even if on a reduced scale, had gone on much as in peace time. In the summer of 1940 the town acted as a temporary receiving centre for men evacuated from Dunkirk; after that it was not long before hotels were rapidly filling up, not with paying guests, but with men and women in uniform. Requisitioned by the War Office, stripped of most furniture and carpets, provided with Army issue beds and chairs and with the curtains replaced by efficient black-outs, they were used as billets for members of the Royal Army Pay Corps, the Pioneer Corps, and the A.T.S.

The *Ilfracombe* hotel itself was taken over by the Warwick office of the Royal Army Pay Corps; every room, from the smallest bedroom high under the roof to the ballroom, was occupied by uniformed clerks of both sexes. The last echoes of Victorian and Edwardian opulence faded into silence as Army boots and heavy service shoes thudded up and down carpetless stairs to which boards had been nailed to reduce wear. Each evening when the offices emptied a guard— unarmed, however—was mounted on the building. The tennis courts near the hotel became a parade ground. At week-ends and in the evenings most of the customers in the town's pubs, theatres, cinemas and cafes wore khaki.

Hidden in the shadow of its hills and never touched by bombing, Ilfracombe often had to watch the brilliant night-time pyrotechnics, beautiful to look at but terrible in significance, on the far shore of the Bristol Channel, as Swansea was set alight with incendiaries.

The Campbell pleasure steamers had once again been diverted to active service. Several, converted to mine-sweepers, sailed under new names. After spending the months of the 'phoney war' keeping the waters of the North Sea clear of mines, seven took part in the evacuation of British and Allied forces from Dunkirk. In these operations the *Brighton Belle,* the *Brighton Queen,* and the *Devonia* were lost—in each case after successfully rescuing many hundreds of men. The surviving steamers went back to mine-sweeping for 18 months, during which time the *Waverley* was sunk by German bombers off Sunderland. The paddlers that remained performed a variety of duties during the final years of the war: as anti-aircraft vessels, as guard or escort ships, and as accommodation ships off the Normandy beaches after the D-day landings in June 1944. Before the war ended one more steamer was lost: the *Glen Avon* foundered in a gale in September 1944, near the mouth of the Seine.

When the remnant of the Campbell fleet was released from naval duties, the *Cambria* and the *Westward Ho!* were in such a bad state that they had to be scrapped. It was possible to refit just three for excursions in 1946—the *Ravenswood,* the *Britannia,* and the *Glen Usk*; in addition, remarkably in that time of shortages, Campbells were able to take delivery of a new paddle-steamer, the *Bristol Queen,* in the autumn of that year. She had been ordered, it seems, the moment the war in Europe was over, and built in less than a year by Charles Hill of Bristol. Grahame Farr says that she may be looked on as representing 'the ultimate in paddler design'.[5] When she sailed majestically down the coasts of Somerset and North Devon on her maiden voyage on 14 September 1946, carrying more than 600 passengers, her approach to Ilfracombe was greeted by the jubilant firing of rockets. Although it was more than 12 months since the surrender of Japan had finally ended the war, it was still a period of austerity and rationing: no doubt the appearance of a fine new paddle-steamer gave a promise of a return to easier times.

Chapter Fourteen

CHANGES ON ALL SIDES

IN ONE RESPECT, the summer season of 1946 was similar to that of 1919: early in April, holiday bookings were reported to be a record for the time of year. But there was a major difficulty: many hotels were still requisitioned by the War Office, and at least one by the Navy. As the Pay Office showed itself in no hurry to move back to Warwick, the *Ilfracombe* hotel was still in effect a block of offices, while many buildings continued to function as billets, instead of preparing to welcome visitors.

Although the Council anticipated in August 1946 the early release of the *Ilfracombe* hotel, and proposals for its future use included its revival as a first-class hotel or its conversion to an orchestral hall,[1] there were those who considered that the Pay Corps' continued presence in the town would be of great benefit. In November the Council decided to press for it not to leave; it was pointed out that no fewer than 135 civilian clerks were by this time working alongside those in uniform, and that the Army spent considerable sums—estimates varied from £2,000 to £4,000—each week. A councillor declared that during the past seven years great prosperity had been enjoyed as the result of the military occupation.

But before long the Pay Corps had gone, and from the beginning of 1947 until early in 1950 the Council discussed at intervals what to do with the hotel. Finally they let it to a large brewery firm, who promptly re-named it the *Holiday Inn,* to the consternation of the Council. Since they had no control over what the lessees might choose to call it, the *Holiday Inn* it remained, despite protests. Only the lower part of the building was used; in the empty and neglected upper rooms, a fatal process of decay was allowed to begin.

A decision about the former tennis courts of the hotel was more easily reached. Taken over by the Council in the 1930s, they had been used as a parade ground all through the war. Now, happily, it was thought best to re-design the area as a public garden, in keeping with the Southern Slope above, and by May 1949 work on this was finished.

During the war, parts of the promenade pier had been demolished as an anti-invasion precaution, and in the late 1940s the whole structure was declared unsafe.[2] Rebuilding took three years, the same length of time as the original construction work 80 years earlier, and cost £60,000. The gang of men, mostly local, allotted to it was not large; the chairman of the Harbour Committee remarked that it had never exceeded 25, and that they had 'encountered

enormous difficulties', sometimes working night and day. In June 1952 the
new pier was opened by Lord Fortescue, and appropriately enough the first vessel
to moor alongside was a paddle-steamer, the *Glen Usk.* At the time, P. and A.
Campbell's manager estimated that between 1896 and 1951 some six million
people had been landed from the company's steamers at Ilfracombe pier.

But whereas the first structure had sturdily withstood wind and weather since
mid-Victorian times, the new one needed some remedial work in only 10 years;
again, in 1974, when as the result of local government reorganisation it came
into the possession of the North Devon District Council, it was said to be in
urgent need of repair. Sadly, by that time the fortunes of P. and A. Campbell
were in decline. Although in the 1960s they began to operate such things as a
hovercraft ferry across the Bristol Channel from Penarth to Weston-super-Mare,
and combined steamer and coach trips along both the north and the south coasts
of Wales and parts of north Devon, and had in addition linked up with Townsend
Car Ferries to offer no-passport day trips to France and Belgium from ports on
the south and south-east coasts of England, by the end of the decade the firm's
paddle-steamer fleet had dwindled away. The *Glen Gower* had been broken up
in 1960, the *Glen Usk* in 1963, and the *Cardiff Queen,* launched as recently as
1947, was offered for sale in 1966. By 1967 only the *Bristol Queen* and the
Westward Ho! (the last Campbell steamer of that name, formerly the Isle of Wight
ferry *Vecta*) were running excursions in the Bristol Channel and calling at
Ilfracombe.

Within a few years those, too, had been withdrawn and their places taken by the
M.V. *Balmoral,* which could carry 600 passengers. In the 1979 season Campbells
still advertised a large number of sailings from Ilfracombe: the long-established
day trips to Lundy continued on three days a week; there were trips to Lynmouth
once a week, morning and afternoon cruises along the coasts of north Devon and
Somerset, excursions to Penarth, Weston-super-Mare and Clovelly, as well as a
regular service to the Mumbles and Swansea. But in the following year the firm
wound up operations. For the 1981 season the *Balmoral* and the *Devonia* were run
by another undertaking; then both ships were put up for sale, and Ilfracombe
found itself, for the first time since the early 19th century, without a regular
passenger service to South Wales and Bristol by sea, and with no day trips to
Lundy and other places to offer to its summer visitors. Lundy's supply ship, the
Polar Bear, was still based in Ilfracombe harbour, and could take a few passengers,
but these were usually holiday-makers intending to spend a week or more in one
of the island's cottages. Those who wanted a day on the island had to travel to
Hartland for an expensive helicopter flight.

Just two sea-going paddle-steamers were still in existence in 1981. Based in
Glasgow and owned by the Waverley Steam Navigation Company, they sailed
south to visit places on the west coast of England. Unfortunately one of them, the
Prince Ivanhoe, ran aground and was written off. A solitary survivor, her owners
now bearing the name of the Waverley Preservation Society, the *Waverley* visited
Ilfracombe a number of times. (In June 1982 the *Western Morning News*
published a photograph of her moored near the ketch *Irene.* The latter was

presumably the vessel built at Bridgwater in 1907 and still in work until 1960; she was later bought and lovingly restored by a London doctor.) The following summer she arrived again and made three trips to Lundy, and one afternoon cruise, between 9 and 12 June.

Meanwhile the railway had already gone. 'May the Rails of the New Line Never Rust!' a banner had proclaimed at the joyful opening in 1874; in less than a century they had not merely rusted, but been ripped up. In the immediate post-war years this would still have seemed an unlikely loss: in September 1946, for instance, at Ilfracombe station, one of the Southern Railway's new loco-motives, especially designed to cope with Devon gradients, was formally named *Ilfracombe* (Bideford and Barnstaple held similar ceremonies for eponymous engines on the same day).[3] In 1948 the *Atlantic Coast Express* service, which had first run from Waterloo to Ilfracombe and other Devon termini in 1926, was restored a year after the introduction of another service, the *Devon Belle*, a Pullman express. However, the *Devon Belle* had only seven years of existence, and although the *Atlantic Coast Express* had a longer life, it ran for the last time on 5 September 1964, the day on which steam trains ceased working on the Exeter to Ilfracombe line, to be replaced by diesels. The Ilfracombe goods yard closed down and the big turntable a short distance away, under the shadow of the Cairn, where generations of children had watched in fascination as the huge locomotives were majestically swung through 180 degrees for their return journey, was taken away. Finally, on 20 October 1970, the Barnstaple to Ilfracombe line was closed.

At the opening of the promenade pier in 1873, speakers had brushed aside fears that rail and sea would compete to each other's detriment, and suggested that they would instead complement one another. It would have been difficult to foresee then that by the late 20th century Ilfracombe would be compelled to rely exclusively on road transport.

After standing empty for several years, the station was bought as the site of a factory making various kinds of filtering equipment. Pall Europe, Ltd., was reported to have been attracted by the clean air of the area. By that time the Cairn was no longer the well-maintained and much-used pleasure ground it had been until the Second World War. Neglected and overgrown, it was becoming a problem for the Ilfracombe Urban District Council. They sought the advice of the Devon Trust for Nature Conservation, which decided that the 19-acre hill would make a good nature reserve, and in March 1974 leased it from the Council, although local government changes meant that before the end of the year the North Devon District Council had become their landlords. For the next four years the Trust was content to survey and record the wild life of the reserve, and to prepare a management plan. In 1978 the hard work of clearing the tangles of bramble, gorse, thorn and saplings that had clogged the paths began; in addition there was the repair or renewal of fences, hedges, gates and seats and the rebuilding of a derelict shelter on Cairn Top. Many volunteers, includ-ing groups of children from Ilfracombe School, gave their time to the tasks. Pall Europe came to an informal agreement with the Devon Trust to allow a four-acre field in their possession, adjoining the reserve, to be managed as a meadow habitat, in which more than 70 flowering plants had been recorded (in the reserve as a whole the total was over 200).

The sudden violent gale of December 1981 and the great frost of January 1982 destroyed a large part of the woodland, but once again volunteers were happy to labour to make the paths safe for everyone who wanted to visit and explore. And if there is no possibility that the railway may be re-opened, as many enthusiasts hoped it might in the days after its closure, at least part of the disused track, a three-mile stretch running as far as Lee Road Bridge, near Mortehoe, has been added to the reserve.[4]

As the Local Board of Health of 1851 had given away to the Ilfracombe Urban District Council in 1894, so, 80 years later, the Urban District Council found itself transformed into the Ilfracombe Town Council, with a diminished degree of authority under the North Devon District Council. The medieval office of portreeve had lapsed long since, but one right acquired by the new Town Council was that of electing a mayor; the first mayor chosen was the chairman of the Council, Mr. Eric James.

In this year of reorganisation many people, not only in Ilfracombe and Devon generally, but elsewhere, were dismayed to learn that the *Ilfracombe* hotel (its re-naming as the *Holiday Inn* had always seemed an anomaly) was said to be in need of very expensive repairs which its usefulness did not justify: it was to be demolished. By this time both the attractive Victorian bandstand and the last vestige of the glass and iron Winter Gardens, erected to celebrate Victoria's Golden Jubilee, had already been swept away. The Victoria Pavilion of 1925 was now flanked by two concrete-walled rectangles, one in use as a bar and the other as a public rest room. Having been unable to prevent these losses, many people resolved not to let the hotel go without a fight. Early in 1974 there had been talk of a consortium, backed by a mysterious financier, which had prepared a scheme for the redevelopment of the hotel buildings to include a dance hall and conference room, skating rink, solarium, bars, and a restaurant. But the money was not forthcoming, and another plan, prepared by a young Ilfracombe architect, Paul Weatherbed, for the conversion of the hotel to a leisure centre, did not gain support from the North Devon District Council.

All through 1975 conflicting arguments were put forward by those who wanted to preserve the building and those who wanted to pull it down. The demolitionists included the local Chamber of Commerce, the Hoteliers' Association, the Small Hotel and Guest House Owners' Association, the Trades Council, Ilfracombe Town Council, and the North Devon District Council. The preservationists had the support of the Society for the Protection of Ancient Buildings, the Ilfracombe Architectural and Preservation Society, the Barnstaple Civic Society, and the Victorian Society. In addition, more than 16,000 people signed a petition against demolition.

A public enquiry was held; it lasted three days. A letter from Sir John Betjeman was read out; he was quoted as saying that the hotel was as important to the image of Ilfracombe as were the towers of the Liver Building to Merseyside.

Ilfracombe was unique because it was less spoiled than other towns, and the hotel itself was bold, harmonious and picturesque on the skyline; he considered that it would be old-fashioned and reactionary of the Council to destroy such a part of the town's heritage. But destroy it they did; the pride of that mid-Victorian consortium, the Ilfracombe Hotel and Esplanade Company, was battered and bulldozed away in the autumn of 1976; walled gardens replaced it, and holiday-makers may sit in the sun where once leisured Victorians and Edwardians ate their meals of many courses, or danced in an elegant ballroom, or took coffee and talked with their friends. The baths where Professor Parker and Miss McGarrick gave exhibitions of swimming to the strains of a band were demolished and the site levelled as a car park.[5] One undoubted advantage was that the area between the end of the Runnacleave ridge and the Capstone offered, for the first time for 110 years, an unobstructed view of the Bristol Channel.

The 1960s and 1970s saw a growing demand for self-catering holidays; to satisfy it a number of small hotels and boarding houses were converted into holiday flats, while so-called holiday villages were developed on the hills to the south of the town—one of them being built on the site of an attractive little zoo that had been run for nearly 20 years after the war in the grounds of Comyn Hill House. Surrounding green slopes rapidly disappeared under rows of bungalows and houses. The value of these hillsides as building land is demonstrated by the fact that in 1975, for instance, six acres in the Crofts Lea area on the Old Barnstaple Road, with outline planning permission for 50 to 60 houses, was sold to a property developer (as usual, not a local firm) for £120,000, and a newspaper report remarked that 'it was expected that many of the houses would be sold to buyers from the London area'.[6] In common with many parts of the south west, Ilfracombe found that large numbers of buyers of dwellings of all kinds (including second homes) came from elsewhere than Devon. The fact that a fairly high proportion of the new permanent residents were retired people began to cause some concern. In 1977 it was reported, under the heading 'Ilfracombe closes its shutters to more old folk', that North Devon's Social Services Department was opposing plans for the conversion of a hotel to yet another home for the elderly; the North Devon Community Action Group carried out a survey which showed that 30 per cent. of the population of the town (which had increased in the decade between the national censuses of 1961 and 1971 by over 1,100) were pensioners.[7]

And if there were more elderly people, there were also a considerable number entitled to claim unemployment benefit. The underlying reasons for this may have been similar to those obtaining in some other seaside towns relying largely on tourism, but the official response was to introduce more manufacturing industry. There was already the factory on the old railway station site, and another near Bicclescombe Park, but it was now decided to leapfrog up to the higher ground east of Mullacott Cross, two miles out of Ilfracombe itself. The Ilfracombe Industrial Development Committee sent out brochures inviting industrialists to take up sites, and the first factories were opened on the estate

35. The *Ilfracombe Hotel*, demolished in 1976; this engraving from Gadsby
shows it a year after its completion in 1867.

in 1978. However, the effect on unemployment was apparently slight, and at the
beginning of 1983 a new scheme was proposed.

As long ago as 1828 someone had evidently suggested enlarging the port of
Ilfracombe in a novel manner: Thomas Cornish wrote, 'If ultimately a floating
harbour should be constructed and completed, we venture to predict that Ilfracombe will not remain long at their Honour's Board under the heading "third
class port"'. Now, in January 1983, the M.P. for North Devon, Tony Speller,
put forward a plan for quadrupling the size of the harbour by means of floating
piers and pontoons extending north-east from the existing promenade pier. The
European M.P. for Devon, Lord O'Hagan, visited Ilfracombe to hear details. An
Ilfracombe Harbour Development Association was formed, and during the
remainder of the year the local press reported at intervals on the numerous bodies
whose interest was being sought, among them Wimpey, McAlpine, Cunard
Brocklebank, Shell Mex and a number of business firms in South Wales. It was
even suggested that '£4 million Arab money should be ploughed into Ilfracombe',[8]
and under the heading 'New harbour lures moguls' it was announced that the
chief executive of the North Devon District Council had been authorised to seek
backers for the scheme in 'the super league money markets of the City of
London'.[9] At the same time, grants were to be requested from the Government
and the E.E.C.

All kinds of benefits were claimed for the proposals: that in some unexplained way they would halve unemployment at a stroke; would provide a marina for some 500 small craft and thus at the same time increase work in service industries associated with sailing; would make possible a resident fishing fleet; and, finally, would provide a shelter for a lifeboat permanently afloat. In addition, it was suggested that Larkstone beach on the south side of the outer harbour could become a landing-place for a roll-on roll-off ferry service between Ilfracombe and South Wales, and that the former site of the *Ilfracombe* hotel should be built on once again to provide a conference and leisure centre complex. A viability study was prepared by the Wimpey Group, and what by some subtle distinction was called a feasibility study was requested from the North Devon District Council.

A ferry-landing on Larkstone—once Laston, where ships unloaded ballast—would involve the building of a service road, and lip service was paid to the need to examine the considerable environmental impact of this: 'landscaping' was mentioned. The inner harbour, it was claimed, would remain untouched, though in view of the traffic likely to be generated, firstly by the construction work, and secondly by the new harbour itself, this seems hardly likely.

Possibly, therefore, the future of Ilfracombe, like that of so many English towns in the past 30 years, is to be placed in the hands of the moguls, magnates, and multi-nationals, the civil servants and the development companies, with unforeseeable effects on both the town and its hinterland. It does not seem surprising that large sums of money, amounting to several million pounds, are said to be necessary to carry out the harbour extension, whether it is to be done by floating piers or pontoons or by more stable structures. As recently as the 1970s, it was found necessary to build a new sea defence wall at Cheyne Beach, at a reported cost of £600,000, to prevent the possible destruction of houses on the Quay and serious damage to the Quay itself; this was completed in 1980. For 'Sir Bourchier's Winds' still at times rouse themselves to hurl the great Atlantic surges upon the coast; and while it may be imagined that the ghosts of generations of Sir Bourchier Wreys, and their ancestors, the Fitzwarrens, would fully approve the idea of an enlarged harbour, they might also watch with deep interest the way it was to be made, from their ancient knowledge of the force of the seas that for centuries have torn at the rocks of Lantern Hill and the base of massive Hillsborough.

APPENDIX

I would like to express my thanks to all the people who kindly responded to my request, published in the *North Devon Advertiser,* for a copy of 'Dear Old Ilfracombe'. Some telephoned and dictated the words of this song (and were even able to sing it, perhaps 70 years after first learning it as children); some lent individual copies of this and other songs by H. Verne, and also some by Allen T. Hussell and W. H. Coates. I am particularly grateful to Mr. P. H. G. Bagshaw of Lee for lending me a copy of the collected edition of Verne's songs, published as *Souvenir Songs of North Devon,* and to Mr. Mervyn C. Dalling, of Swimbridge, for lending Hussell and Coates' song 'Coachman Sam'.

DEAR OLD ILFRACOMBE

Words and music by H. Verne. Published in 1905 by J. T. White, who had shops in Barnstaple, Ilfracombe and Bideford

'Twas many and many a year ago,
The hunt at an end and the sun getting low,
And miles from his home at the end of the day
The squire of Brendon had lost his way,
Lost his way, well-a-day.
But a kirtle of red in the gloom he espied,
'Heigh-ho, pretty maid', he gaily cried,
'Where on earth does this rugged old pathway go?'
And a sweet voice answered, 'What, don't you know?
Don't you know?
Why, right through Chambercombe down into Ilfracombe,
Grandest old place in the world it be,
Though it's just a few cottages,
Homes of the fisherfolk,
Dear old Ilfracombe by the sea'.

How strange that so often on stag-hunting day
The end of the run should be Chambercombe way,
And the kirtle of red in the dusk should appear
Which the arms of the Squire went round, I fear,
Round I fear, dear oh dear!
But the Ilfracombe fishermaid came to be
The lady of Brendon, oh don't you see,
But she never forsook her old friends below,
And for years and years with her lord would go,
As they know,
Why, right through Chambercombe down into Ilfracombe,
Dear old Ilfracombe by the sea.

121

36.   The front cover of the musical score of 'Dear Old Ilfracombe'.

DEAR OLD ILFRACOMBE.

SONG OF DEVON, № 2.

Written and Composed by

H. VERNE.

'Twas ma-ny and ma-ny a year a-go, The hunt was at end and the sun get-ting low, And miles from his home at the

(E♭)

H. 1931.

37. The first page of the musical score of 'Dear Old Ilfracombe'.

Of Verne's other songs, 'Clovelly' (also 1905) has two verses of fairly conventional nostalgia of the 'far from home' variety:

> 'Clovelly, ah sweet Clovelly
> . . . when I wander sad and friendless
> In lands a thousand leagues away
> I long and long for my returning
> . . . Clovelly, ah sweet Clovelly, adieu, adieu.'

'Watersmeet' (again 1905) is simply a celebration of the

> 'Fairest spot in fair Devonia,
> In the valley soft and sweet
> Where the little moorland rivers
> Like a pair of lovers meet . . .
>
> In my dreams and in my waking
> Till my heart has ceased to beat
> Memory will link together
> Summer, Youth and Watersmeet.'

'The Witches of Lyn' (1908) which, according to the song sheet, was 'written expressly for Miss Hope Jackson', belongs to the tradition of folk ballads: the first witch, 'A blear-eyed crone in a gruesome den' in the Valley of Rocks, is visited by a sportive lad who offers her a silver groat to learn his fortune, only to be told,

> 'Silver but pays for a broken heart,
> Gold shall your doom begin,
> For the moon, one night, on your face will shine,
> In the bed of the silver Lyn.'

The second witch, 'so young and so fair' who lives in the valley below, then lays her spell on the lad.

> 'I bring you my love and my life!' he cried,
> 'Oh what is my fate to be?'

Inevitably, the girl spurns him:

> 'Your gifts bestow on some maiden low
> For a lord and his gold I win.'
> And the moon that night on his dead face shone
> In a pool of the silver Lyn.'

One other song by Verne, 'The Path to Lee', is known; this was published in 1914 as *Song of Devon No. 5*. Unfortunately it seems impossible to discover anything about Verne himself. He was probably a Devon visitor rather than a Devonian. Kelly's *Directories* for the 1900s do not show anyone of the name of Verne living in any of the principal towns of north Devon.

If, in Edwardian days, Verne's first four songs were, as the front cover of the souvenir collection claimed, 'Always enthusiastically received at Ilfracombe Band Concerts', those of Allen Hussell and Will Coates were probably listened to with enjoyment in the years after the First World War. Among these were 'The Vale of Fuchsias (Dear little Lee)' and 'Coachman Sam'. 'The Vale of Fuchsias', like Verne's 'Watersmeet', has all the sentiment of its period, with a refrain

> 'Fair little valley, down by the sea
> Home of the fuchsia, haunt of the bee;
> Waking or dreaming, I think of thee
> Sweet vale of fuchsias, dear little Lee.'

But by contrast with Verne's 'Clovelly', it looks towards a happy ending:

> 'With my love I would dwell where the sweet fuchsias bloom,
> There's a little thatched cottage with just enough room,
> With the song of the birds, and the song of the sea,
> Ever happy I'd be down at dear little Lee.'

Both 'The Vale of Fuchsias' and 'Coachman Sam' were published by Henry T. Meredith (formerly O. Nicklin and Sons) at the Music Warehouse, Ilfracombe, and by Warren and Phillips, 150 Victoria Street, London.

Allen Hussell was an architect by profession; Will Coates was a shopkeeper who worked, as a young man, as an assistant in the shop of Mr. Cole, on the corner of Portland Street, in which Ilfracombe's 'great fire' began in 1896. Both were local men, and would have known Sam Colwill well.

COACHMAN SAM

> I'll sing you a song of the olden days,
> The coaching days, the golden days,
> Of Coachman Sam and his team of greys
> On the Lynton road in the morning;
> Our Sam was happy, blithe and gay,
> Happy he as the birds in May,
> For with tale and song he beguil'd the way
> On the Lynton road in the morning [last two lines repeated].
> Then sing Heigh Ho! for the olden days,
> The rollicking, galloping coaching days,
> And sing Heigh Ho! for Sam and his greys
> On the Lynton road in the morning.
>
> Sam's team was the pride of the West Countrie,
> That fair countrie, my dear countrie,
> And never a grander drive there be
> Than the Lynton road in the morning;
> It winds along by the deep blue sea,
> Past valley and rock, green meadow and tree,
> The horn's merry notes rang cheerily
> O'er the Lynton road in the morning [repeat last two lines and
>   refrain 'Then sing Heigh Ho! . . . On the Lynton road in the
>   morning'].

COACHMAN SAM

"On the Lynton road in the morning"

Song

Words by
WILL. H. COATES

Music by
ALLEN T. HUSSELL

Composer of
"The Riderless Steed"
"Sir Reynard" &c.

Price
1/6 net cash.

Published by
HENRY T. MEREDITH,
(formerly O. Nicklin & Sons)
"The Music Warehouse"
Ilfracombe.

London:
WARREN & PHILLIPS,
150, Victoria Street, S.W.

38. The front cover of the musical score of 'Coachman Sam'.

COACHMAN SAM.
Song.

Words by
WILL. H. COATES.

Music by
ALLEN T. HUSSELL.

sing you a song of the old-en days, The coach-ing days, the gold-en days, Of

Coach-man Sam and his team of greys, On the Lyn-ton road in the morn - ing: Our

O'N. & S. 3.

39. The first page of the musical score of 'Coachman Sam'.

But gone, alas! are the olden days,
The dear old, good old coaching days,
No more will Sam and his team of greys
Take the Lynton road in the morning.
In the old churchyard he lies at rest
And we mourn his loss in the golden West,
For he was of coachmen the first and best
On the Lynton road in the morning [repeat refrain].

The 'horn's merry notes' were real enough: Sam Colwill maintained the tradition of the stage coach driver he had once been; his fanfare was a familiar sound on the Ilfracombe to Lynton run. His coach horn and his whip are both to be seen in the Ilfracombe museum, together with the horn of his rival, Mr. Copp.

NOTES

Chapter One

1. L. V. Grinsell, *The Archaeology of Exmoor* (David and Charles, 1970), p. 79.
2. L. V. Grinsell, *op. cit.*, p. 96, and Aileen Fox, *South West England* (Thames and Hudson, 1964).
3. J. J. Alexander, *Transactions of the Devonshire Association*, Vol. 69, pp. 209–210, and Gower, Mawer and Stenton, *Place Names of Devon* (C.U.P., 1931).
4. C. E. Champernowne, 'A History of the Champernowne Family' (typescript, North Devon Athenaeum, 1954).
5. H. P. R. Finberg, 'The Boroughs of Devon' (*Devon and Cornwall Notes and Queries*, Vol. 24, 1951).
6. Revd. O. J. Reichel, *The Hundreds of Devon* (Devonshire Association).
7. Allen T. Hussell, *North Devon Churches* (Barnstaple, 1909).
8. The full list of names was : Roberte de Bikeleghe, Adami de Stoddone, Wilhelmi Schurreve (Shire Reeve?) and Richardi Schurreve, Johannis le Lange, Adami de Trewent, Thome de Trewent, Wilhelmi le Tailleur, Adami Fabri, Thome Ware, Wilhelmi Gersome, Wilhelmi Benet, junioris, Rogeri Mugge, Johannis Henri, Johannis Knosse, Johelis Fabri, Johannis Pistoris, Thome Pistoris, 'et nonullorum'.
9. W. G. Hoskins, *Old Devon* (David and Charles, 1966).
10. 'In capella St Nicholai super Portum Ville de Ilfracombe fundata, luminare quoddam singulis annis per totum hiemen nocturnis temporibus in summitate dicte capella ardens, velut Stella nocte choruscans invenitur.'

Chapter Two

1. W. G. Hoskins, *Devon* (David and Charles, 1954), p. 546.
2. Audrey M. Erskine, 'The Devonshire Lay Subsidy of 1332' (*Devon and Cornwall Record Society*, 1969).
3. These books, *The Golden Legend* and *The Pupil of the Eye*, were manuals of theology much studied in the Middle Ages. *The Golden Legend*, also known as the 'Lombardia Historica', contains lives of saints and short treatises about Christian festivals. It was drawn up by Jacob of Voragne between 1255 and 1266. Caxton translated and published an edition, but this would have been 20 years or more after Morton's death, which would mean that his copy was in manuscript; it must have been of considerable value at a time when books of any kind were scarce.
4. Dorothy M. Gardiner (ed.), 'A Calendar of Early Chancery Proceedings relating to West Country Shipping, 1388–1483' (*Devon and Cornwall Record Society*, 1976).
5. T. L. Stoate (ed.), *Devon Subsidy Rolls, 1524–1527* (published privately, Bristol, 1979), and *A Survey of West Country Manors* (also published privately, Bristol, 1979).
6. T. L. Stoate (ed.), *The Devon Muster Roll for 1569* (published privately, Bristol, 1977). Holinshed's *Chronicle* contains an account by William Harrison of the typical armour and weaponry of the Elizabethan man; although the long bow was largely 'given over', he says that 'our countrymen wax skilful in sundry other points, as in shooting in small pieces, the caliver,

the handling of the pike, in the several uses whereof they are become very expert. Our armour differeth not from that of other nations, and therefore consisteth of corselets, almain rivets, shirts of mail, jacks quilted and covered over with fustian or canvas, over thick plates of iron that are sewed in the same, and of which there is no town or village that hath not her convenient furniture . . . kept in one several place of every town, appointed by the consent of the whole parish, where it is always ready to be had and worn within an hour's warning . . . almost no village so poor in England (be it never so small) that hath not sufficient furniture in a readiness to set forth three or four soldiers, as one archer, one gunner, one pike and a billman at the very least'.

7. 'Bristol Channel Shipping: cross-channel voyages between Welsh ports and those in North Devon and Somerset recorded in the Welsh Port Books, 1560–1603' (North Devon Athenaeum typescript).

8. William Laird Clowes, *A History of the Navy*, Vol. I (Sampson Low, Marston and Co., 1897).

Chapter Three

1. Revd. Frank Nesbitt, *Ilfracombe Parish Church* (Ilfracombe, 1906).

2. Thomas Wainwright, who transcribed the parish registers, read 'zealous pastor' instead of 'precious pastor'.

3. It seems unlikely that the road from Combe Martin ever passed under the site of Quayfield House, which stands on the south side of the harbour and only a short distance from it. However, a painting of 1805 shows a small fort-like building on the summit of what is still known as Castle Hill, with a second similar building some distance down the slope.

4. R. W. Cotton, *Barnstaple and the Northern Part of Devonshire during the Great Civil War, 1642–1646* (London, 1889).

Chapter Four

1. John Longhurst, 'The Port of Ilfracombe', *Ilfracombe and Lee, Some Aspects of their History* (Ilfracombe Local History Society, 1978).

2. W. J. Slade and Basil Greenhill, *West Country Coasting Ketches* (Conway Maritime Press, 1974).

3. Grahame Farr, 'Shipbuilding in North Devon' (National Maritime Musuem Monograph, No. 22, 1976).

4. M. M. Oppenheim, *Maritime History of Devon* (University of Exeter, 1968). According to Sir Sherston Baker, *The Office of Vice-Admiral of the Coast* (London, 1884), there were 19 vice-admiralties in all, one for each of the maritime counties of England, each responsible to a Lord Admiral, with the duty of carefully looking into 'all things that are ordained by the Lord Admiral, and yearly to keep a court in their several counties where every man's complaint may be publicly heard'. They had jurisdiction over 'Sea shores and Public Streams, Ports, Freshwaters, River Creeks and Arms as well of the Sea as of Rivers and Coasts'.

5. Michael Bouquet, *West Country Sail* (David and Charles, 1971).

6. J. R. Chanter and Thomas Wainwright, *Reprint of the Barnstaple Records*, Vol. II, pp. 173–4 (Barnstaple, 1900).

7. Grahame Farr, *op. cit.*

8. *Devon and Cornwall Notes and Queries*, Vol. I, pp. 176–77.

9. Grahame Farr, *op. cit.*

Chapter Five

1. Lansdowne MSS. 1152.

2. William Laird Clowes, *op. cit.*, Vol. IV.

3. Philip Rogers Webber, 1732–1819. J.P. and Deputy Lieutenant of Devon. Private diary, quoted by kind permission of Colonel G. S. Incledon-Webber.

4. The proclamation was published by Syle, a bookseller and printer of Barnstaple.

5. Miss May Down, the last surviving member of the family, who had served in the W.R.N.S. during the First World War, died in Ilfracombe in February 1975.

6. There is a tradition that Nelson himself visited Ilfracombe, staying at the *Britannia* hotel, though there is no documentary evidence for this. He certainly visited Devon; in January 1801, having been promoted Vice-Admiral of the Blue, he was ordered to hoist his flag in the *San Josef* at Plymouth, under Lord St Vincent. On 21 January he was at Exeter, where he received the freedom of the city; three days later Plymouth, too, made him a freeman.

There are other places where he is reputed to have stayed, again without its being possible to find confirmation, and there are periods of his life—especially during his 'five years on the beach', from December 1787, when he was paid off the *Boreas* until January 1793, when he was appointed Captain of the *Agamemnon*—during which his movements are not exactly known. I am indebted to A. W. H. Pearsall, Historian to the National Maritime Museum, for confirming that no known record exists of his having made any visit to Ilfracombe.

7. The *Dictionary of National Biography* gives his date of birth as 1751, but the Ilfracombe parish registers show that his baptism was registered on 9 December 1750.

8. The *Devon Protestation Returns* of 1641 show 322 signatories. As these would all have been men over the age of 18, multiplication by a factor of 3.5 gives a possible population of 1,127.

9. From an Act of 1815 'for procuring returns to the Expence and Maintenance of the Poor in England, also relative to the Highways', it is possible to learn that the number of people being permanently relieved from the Poor Rate in Ilfracombe, in 1813, was 46 in the workhouse and 71 out; in 1814, 42 in the workhouse, 68 out; in 1815, 37 in the workhouse, 79 out. The total assessment of 'real property' for the purposes of property tax in 1815 was £7,547.

10. T. H. Stoate, *A Survey of West Country Manors, op. cit.*

11. Devon Record Office, P.O. 1: Account book of Workhouse expenses and in relief, 1724–1748; P.O. 2: Account Book of Workhouses expenses and in relief, 1748–1757; P.O. 3: Account Book of Workhouse expenses in relief, 1757–1767; P.O. 4: Account Book of Workhouse expenses and in and out relief, 1767–1777; P.O. 5: Account Book of Casual Poor Relief and out relief, 1749–1763; P.O. 6: Account Book of Casual Poor Relief and out relief, 1763–1774; P.O. 7: Account Book 'Poor Book', September 1787–1788; P.V. 1: Vestry Minute Book, 1740–1813.

12. In the parish registers appears a list of children born in Ilfracombe between the years 1727 and 1759 who 'had not been baptised according to the form nor by the minister of the Church of England' but 'according to the form of the presbyterians'. Three of John Tawman's children were entered as having been baptised 'in ye presbyterian meeting house in Ilfracombe'.

Chapter Six

1. W. G. Hoskins, *Devon*, p. 248.

2. The Revd. Chichester Wrey was one of the executors of her will, and in view of the Wrey family's association with Ilfracombe, it is possible that he had some influence on Gertrude Pincombe's decision. She was a considerable property owner, with estates in Devon and Somerset.

3. 'Report of the Commissioners concerning Charities for Devon', 1826.

4. Gratiana Chanter, *Wanderings in North Devon* (Ilfracombe,1887).

5. Although Ilfracombe had some kind of small grammar school at No. 1 Oxford Grove in the late 19th century, it was 1935 before a grammar school to accommodate a large number of pupils was built. A County secondary school was established in 1920. Both were superseded in 1966 by Ilfracombe School and Community College, built at Worth Road.

Chapter Seven

1. All quotations in this chapter are from *The Journals and Letters of Fanny Burney* (Madame d'Arblay), Vol. X, ed. by Warren Derry (O.U.P., 1982).

Chapter Eight

1. According to his obituary in the *North Devon Journal*, Meek was born in 1778, and in 1801 married Mary Down, a daughter of Edward Down, the preventive officer. He became comptroller of the government's victualling and transport services; Sir Robert Peel sent him on a Continental tour in 1841 'to collect statistical information respecting agricultural produce and shipping', and it was to a large extent on his reports that Peel based his Free Trade Bill of 1846. Meek retired in 1850, and was knighted and made a Commander of the Bath the following year. He died at Ilfracombe in May 1856.

2. J. R. Chanter in his *Sketches of a Literary History of Barnstaple*, published in 1865, speaks of Cornish as an 'erratic genius' who had been well known in Barnstaple some 30 years earlier. He served his apprenticeship as a printer there, went to London, and eventually became a partner in a successful printing business. Returning to Barnstaple he established a newspaper, the *North Devon Advertiser and Tiverton Chronicle*, 'but ran into financial difficulties after a year and sold out'. He published one or two books, including *British Melodies* (Smith and Elder, 1832), *The Young Gentleman's Book* of what were described as 'choice readings' (Adam, 1832), and *The Thames*, a collection of verse (Pickering, 1842).

3. *The New British Traveller*, or 'Modern Panorama of England and Wales', Vol. 2 (London, 1819).

4. The original diary is in the Ilfracombe museum. Mervyn G. Palmer, the museum's first curator, transcribed it for publication in the *Transactions of the Devonshire Association* (Vol. 75, pp. 211-243, and Vol. 76, pp. 215-247).

5. This is a puzzling entry. In 1835 the North Devon Mining Company had been the most recent of many such undertakings in Combe Martin; like its predecessors it failed. The mine had closed only the year before Benham's visit. But although the 1851 census was to record the presence in the village of 25 men and women (eight of them Cornish) in some way connected with mining—lead miner, culm miner, lead and silver smelter, mine agent, and so on—in 1849 the only activity was in the smelting house at the mouth of the valley where the washing of umber was carried on.

6. The figures were: 1847, 54; 1848, 62; 1850, 54; 1851, 49.

7. Susan Chitty, *The Beast and the Monk* (Hodder and Stoughton, 1974).

Chapter Nine

1. Charles Creighton, *A History of Epidemics in England* (Cambridge, 1894).

2. *North Devon Journal*, 19 September 1850.

3. Grahame Farr, *Shipbuilding in North Devon, op. cit.*

4. Henry Besley, *The Route Book of Devon* (Exeter, no date, c. 1850).

5. In Kelly's *Directory* for 1889, John Dadd's North Devon Fernery and Rosary claimed to have the largest stocks of British ferns in the kingdom.

6. George Tugwell. Oriel College, Oxford: B.A. 1852, M.A. 1856. Priest, 1862. Curate of Ilfracombe, 1853-68; Perpetual Curate of St Matthew's, Lee, 1869-70; Rector of Bathwick, 1871. Author of: *The Four Seasons of Architecture* (1853); *Woodleigh, or Life and Death* (1855); *The Church in the Household (a Manual of Family Devotion selected from the Book of Common prayer)* (1855); *A Manual of the Sea Anemones commonly found on the British Coast* (1856); *The North Devon Handbook* (1857) (4th edn., 1877); *On the Mountain (North Wales, notes on its Botany, Geology, Fisheries, etc.* (1862); *The North Devon Scenery Book*

(1863); *Arrows* (sermons preached at Bathwick) (1876); *Emblems of the Passion* (1888). It appears to have been Tugwell who first gave currency to the often repeated story of the haunted room at Chambercombe Manor; it occurs in both his *North Devon Handbook* and *North Devon Scenery Book,* as does a brief account of the Doones of Badgworthy, although both books appeared before Blackmore's *Lorna Doone* (the *North Devon Handbook* being 12 years earlier).

7. '. . . the lovely Sea-Anemones, now the ornament of countless drawing rooms, studies, and back parlours, as well as the delight of unnumbered amateurs', G. H. Lewes wrote in *Seaside Studies.* 'In glass tanks and elegant vases of various device, in finger glasses and common tumblers, the lovely creature may be seen expanding its coronal of tentacles, on mimic rocks, amid mimic forests of algae, in mimic oceans of pump water and certain mixtures of chlorides and carbonates, regulated by a "specific gravity test" . . . At once pet, ornament and "subject for dissection", the Sea-Anemone has a well-established popularity in the British family circle . . . Mr. Gosse by his pleasant books, and Mr. Mitchell by his tanks in the Regent's Park Zoological Gardens, have mainly contributed to the diffusion of the enthusiasm.'

Chapter Ten

1. Ilfracombe seems to have employed several town criers at a time during the 19th century; Beatrix Potter speaks of more than one when she visited the town in the early 1880s, and found some amusement in their announcements. Among later town criers were Tom Davie, son of the lighthouse keeper who brought up 13 children in the chapel of St Nicholas—he retired in 1927 at the age of 70 after 35 years as a crier—and R. Martin, who in Edwardian days was a mounted crier, and appeared on local postcards.

2. The Ilfracombe Bank, established in 1807, had occupied this house, but it had a short life, being amalgamated with the National Provincial in 1836.

3. The Sisters of the Immaculate Conception moved to Ilfracombe from Brittany in 1903; they opened their school at Garth House, Torrs Park, in 1907.

4. There are 14 stanzas, written by a local shopkeeper, W. H. Coates, who also wrote the words of several songs which became popular in the years just before and after the First World War (*see* Appendix). According to Coates's account, after the fight Prince Frederick (referred to as the Kaiser, though his father, the Emperor of Germany, was to live another 10 years) turned to Albert Price and said:

> 'Mine Friend! you'll rue the day,
> For what you've done t'mine poor nose,
> Mine word! I'll make you pay.
> I'll build big ships and gurt big guns,
> Then one day I will come
> And blow this place t'smithereens,
> And you—t'kingdom come.'

A copy of the whole piece is to be seen in the Ilfracombe museum.

5. 'Ilfracombe Lifeboats' (R.N.L.I., Ilfracombe, 1978).

6. Grahame Farr, *Wreck and Rescue in the Bristol Channel* (D. Bradford Barton, 1966), Chapter Five.

7. *North Devon Journal,* 15 November 1866.

Chapter Eleven

1. Leslie Linder, *The Journal of Beatrix Potter,* transcribed from her code writings (Frederick Warne and Co., Ltd., 1966).

2. The house she saw dates mainly from 1825, although the Watermouth Estate had been in the possession of the Basset family since 1712.

3. The last vessel to be registered was the *Little Western,* built by George Harris in 1839.

4. W. J. Slade and Basil Greenhill, *West Country Coasting Ketches* (Conway Maritime Press, 1974).

5. Grahame Farr, *Shipbuilding in North Devon, op. cit.*

6. John Besley Gribble, *Memorials of Barnstaple* (Barnstaple, 1830).

7. During the second half of the 19th century the health-giving aspect of the resort was increasingly stressed: in the 1860s the Town Improvement Committee issued a booklet to be sent out to intending visitors with the title 'Ilfracombe, the Healthiest of English Watering Places', and the Medical Officer of Health, Dr. E. F. Slade-King, wrote another which more modestly called it 'Ilfracombe, the Healthiest of Devonshire Watering Places'.

8. Ilfracombe has suffered a number of serious fires in the past 70 or 80 years. Nos. 1 and 2 The Woodlands, Torrs Park, were completely gutted in October 1922, as was the *Grand* hotel in April 1926, and the Ilfracombe Laundry at Chambercombe in 1937. The Victoria Pavilion suffered considerable fire damage in June 1949. As recently as December 1981, a hundred people had to be evacuated from the Portland Street area when Draper's Government Surplus Store caught fire, and only a month before the fire of September 1983, three buildings in Broad Street, including the *Ship and Pilot,* also suffered damage, two girls escaping almost certain death by climbing over roofs.

Chapter Twelve

1. A guide published by the Devonshire Association in 1900, *The Book of Fair Devon,* remarked that 'This town is known for its freshness, and the links keep up the reputation, being 500 to 600 feet above, and distant about one and a half miles. The course is a little over a mile in length, and is a nine-hole. It is full of such difficulties as skilled players like'.

2. These were: John Pile, d. 17.5.1784, aged 100; Sarah Williams (widow), d. 13.1.1788, aged 107; William Soaper, d. 6.11.1804, aged 103; John Davis, d. 4.3.1840, aged 102; Mary Ann Lamb, d. 12.10.1849, aged 100; Elizabeth Brooks, d. 10.1.1858, aged 100; Nanny Vagges (widow), d. 6.10.1859, aged 101; Jane Richards, d. 13.6.1875, aged 101; John Bray, d. 25.1.1897, aged 100; and Mary Louise Lomas, d. 29.6.1913, aged 103.

Chapter Thirteen

1. *Bristol Channel Guide* (F. G. Warne, Bristol, 1933).

2. Grahame Farr, *West Country Passenger Steamers* (T. Stephenson and Sons, Ltd., 1967).

3. *North Devon Journal,* January 1928.

4. R. C. Anderson and G. G. A. Frankis, *A History of Western National* (David and Charles, 1979).

5. Grahame Farr, *West Country Passenger Steamers, op. cit.*

Chapter Fourteen

1. *North Devon Journal-Herald,* 29 August 1946.

2. *North Devon Journal-Herald,* 5 June 1952.

3. *North Devon Journal-Herald,* 5 September 1946.

4. For a detailed account of this part of the Devon Trust's valuable work, *see* Joan Robertson, 'The Cairn, Ilfracombe—the Making of a Reserve', *Nature in Devon* (the Journal of the Devon Trust for Nature Conservation, 1982), from which the above information is drawn.

5. New public baths had already been opened at Hillsborough in 1973.

6. *Western Morning News,* 5 April 1975.

7. *Western Morning News,* 7 April 1977.

8. *North Devon Journal-Herald,* 4 August 1983.

9. *Western Morning News,* 25 February 1983.

BIBLIOGRAPHY

Main Sources

Arber, E. A. Newell, *The Coast Scenery of North Devon* (J. M. Dent, Ltd., 1911).

Bouquet, Michael, *West Country Sail* (David and Charles, Newton Abbot, 1971).

Bowring, D. W., *Ilfracombe Throughout the Ages* (Wheaton and Co., Exeter, 1931).

Burney, Fanny, *The Journals and Letters,* vol. X. Edited by Warren Derry (O.U.P. 1982).

Chanter, Charlotte, *Ferny Combes* (London, 1857).

Chanter, Gratiana, *Wanderings in North Devon* (Twiss and Son, Ilfracombe, 1887).

Chitty, Susan, *The Beast and the Monk* (Hodder and Stoughton, 1974).

Cornish, T. H., *Sketch of the Rise and Progress of the Principal Towns of North Devon* (Bristol, 1828).

Cotton, R. W., *Barnstaple and the Northern Part of Devonshire during the Great Civil War, 1642-1646* (London, 1889).

Eliot, George, 'Recollections of Ilfracombe', and 'How I came to write Fiction', *The George Eliot Letters.* Edited by Gordon S. Haight (Yale U.P., 1979).

Farr, Grahame, *Shipbuilding in North Devon* (National Maritime Museum Monograph, no. 22, 1976); *Ships and Harbours of Exmoor* (Exmoor Press, 1970); *West Country Passenger Steamers* (T. Stephenson and Sons, Ltd., Prescot, 1967); *Wreck and Rescue in the Bristol Channel* (D. Bradford Barton, Truro, 1966).

Gosse, Philip, *A Naturalist's Rambles on the Devonshire Coast* (London, 1853).

Griffin, C. R. J., *A Golden Milestone* (Ilfracombe, 1956).

Grinsell, L. V., *The Archaeology of Exmoor* (David and Charles, Newton Abbot, 1970).

Hoskins, W. G., *Devon* (David and Charles, 1954); *Old Devon* (David and Charles, 1966).

Hussell, Allen T., *North Devon Churches* (Barnstaple, 1909).

Kingsley, Charles, *Prose Idylls, New and Old* (Macmillan, 1889).

Lewes, George Henry, *Seaside Studies at Ilfracombe, Tenby, the Scilly Isles and Jersey* (Blackpool, 1858).

Linder, Leslie, *The Journal of Beatrix Potter, 1881–1897,* transcribed from her code writings (Frederick Warne and Co., Ltd., 1966).

Lysons, Revd. Daniel, *Topographical and Historical Account of Devonshire* (London, 1822).

Maggs, C., *The Barnstaple and Ilfracombe Railway* (Locomotion Papers, no. 111, Oakwood Press, 1978).

Lock, Jim, *The Centenary of the Barnstaple-Ilfracombe Line, 1874–1974* (Aycliffe Press, Barnstaple, 1974).

Nesbitt, Revd. Frank, *Ilfracombe Parish Church* (Ilfracombe, 1906).

Oliver, Revd. George, *Ecclesiastical Antiquities in Devon* (London, 1840).

Oppenheim, M. M., *The Maritime History of Devon* (University of Exeter, 1968).

Risdon, Tristram, *Chorographical Description or Survey of the County of Devon* (London, 1811).

Slade, W. J., and Greenhill, Basil, *West Country Coasting Ketches* (Conway Maritime Press, Greenwich, 1974).

Trevisick, Charles, *My Home is a Zoo* (Stanley Paul, 1976).

White, William, *History, Gazetteer and Directory of Devonshire, 1850* (David and Charles Reprints, 1968).

Wilson, Lilian, *Ilfracombe's Yesterdays* (Barnstaple, 1976).

Worth, R. N., *History of Devon* (London, 1895).

Guide Books

Banfield, J., *A Guide to Ilfracombe, Lynton, Clovelly and the Neighbouring Towns* (Ilfracombe, no date: *c.* 1845).

Besley, H., *The Route Book of Devonshire* (Exeter, no date: *c.* 1850).

Britton, J., and Brayley, E. W., *Devonshire and Cornwall Illustrated* (London, 1832).

Campbell, P. and A., *Bristol Channel Shipping* (F. G. Warne, Bristol, 1933).

Dugdale, James, *The New British Traveller* (London, 1819).

Green, T. R. L., *The Story of Ilfracombe Harbour* (Ilfracombe, 1943).

Lammas, Edwin, *Ilfracombe as it is* (Ilfracombe, 1840).

Slade King, Dr. E. J., *Ilfracombe, the Healthiest Devonshire Watering Place* (2nd edn.) (Ilfracombe, 1875).

Tugwell, Revd. George, *The North Devon Handbook* (London and Ilfracombe, 1857); *The North Devon Scenery Book* (London and Ilfracombe, 1863).

Walters, W., *Ilfracombe, A Health Resort* (Ilfracombe, *c.* 1878).

Worth, R. N., *Tourists' Guide to North Devon* (London, 1879)

United Devon Association, *The Book of Fair Devon* (Exeter, 1899).

Printed Records

Erskine, Audrey M., *The Devon Lay Subsidy of 1332* (Devon and Cornwall Record Society, Torquay, 1969).

Gardiner, Dorothy M., *A Calendar of Early Chancery Proceedings relating to West Country Shipping, 1388–1483* (Devon and Cornwall Record Society, Torquay, 1976).

Howard, A. J., *The Devon Protestation Returns, 1641* (privately printed, 1973).

Stoate, T. L., *The Devon Muster Roll for 1569* (privately printed, Bristol, 1977); *Devon Subsidy Rolls, 1524–1527* (privately printed, Bristol, 1979); *A Survey of West Country Manors* (privately printed, Bristol, 1979).

Essays

Longhurst, John, 'The Port of Ilfracombe', *Ilfracombe and Lee, Some Aspects of their History* (Ilfracombe Local History Society, 1978).
May, Bruce, 'The Rise of Ilfracombe as a seaside resort in the 19th and early 20th centuries'. Exeter Papers in Economic History, no. 13. Edited by Walter Minchinton (Exeter, 1980).

Unpublished Family Histories

Champernowne, Elizabeth, 'The Champernowne Family' (North Devon Athenaeum).
Down, N. C. S., 'Some old Ilfracombe Families and their Houses' (Ilfracombe Museum).

INDEX